FORTRESS 112

DEFENSES OF BERMUDA 1612–1995

**TERRANCE MCGOVERN AND
EDWARD HARRIS**

ILLUSTRATED BY ADAM HOOK

Series Editor Marcus Cowper

Osprey Publishing
c/o Bloomsbury Publishing Inc.
1385 Broadway, 5th Floor, New York, NY 10018, USA
E-mail: info@ospreypublishing.com
www.ospreypublishing.com

OSPREY is a trademark of Osprey Publishing Ltd, a division of Bloomsbury Publishing Plc.

Osprey Publishing supports the Woodland Trust, the UK's leading woodland conservation charity. Between 2014 and 2018 our donations are being spent on their Centenary Woods project in the UK.

To find out more about our authors and books visit www.ospreypublishing.com. Here you will find extracts, author interviews, details of forthcoming events and the option to sign up for our newsletter.

First published in Great Britain in 2018

A CIP catalog record for this book is available from the British Library.

ISBN: PB: 978 1 4728 2596 4
        ePub: 978 1 4728 2598 8
        ePDF: 978 14728 2599 5
        XML: 978 14728 2597 1

18 19 20 21 22   10 9 8 7 6 5 4 3 2 1

Index by Alison Worthington
Typeset in Myriad Pro and Sabon
Maps by Bounford.com
Page layouts by PDQ Digital Media Solutions, Bungay, UK
Printed in China through World Print Ltd.

Front cover:
One of the principal Bermuda defenses of the 1800s, Fort St Catherine in St George was last altered in the 1870s for the emplacement of 10in., 18-ton Rifled Muzzle Loaders (RMLs). Shown from the air in a 1980s photograph, this fort is now a museum open to the public and is one of the most visited fortifications on Bermuda. (NMB Collections)

Page 1:
Lieutenant Gerald Rickards Hughes, West India Regiment, sits astride a camouflaged 11in., 25-ton RML on a garrison carriage at Fort Victoria, in 1902. (NMB Collections)

ABOUT THE AUTHORS

Terrance McGovern has authored five books and numerous articles on fortifications, three of those books being for Osprey's Fortress Series (*American Defenses of Corregidor and Manila Bay 1898–1945*; *Defenses of Pearl Harbor and Oahu 1907–50*; *American Coastal Defenses 1885–1950*). He has also published 11 books on coast defense and fortifications through Redoubt Press or CDSG Press. Terry was Chairman of the US-based Coast Defense Study Group and continues to be a long-time officer. He has also been the editor of the Fortress Study Group annual journal, *FORT*. He is a director of the International Fortress Council and the Council on America's Military Past.

Dr Edward C. Harris, MBE, JP, FSA is a well-known Bermudian archaeologist. He is best known for the Harris Matrix, which is considered by many to be the industry standard, published in 1979 as the *Principles of Archaeological Stratigraphy*. He holds degrees from Columbia University, New York, and University College London, and is a Fellow of the Society of Antiquaries of London. Dr Harris served as the executive director of the National Museum of Bermuda 1980–2017 (www.nmb.bm) and wrote a history column, entitled "Heritage Matters," for the local newspaper for ten years. He also authored *Bermuda Forts 1612–1957*.

AUTHORS' NOTE

This book is dedicated to the preservation of the wonderful fortifications of Bermuda for future generations. We hope this book will encourage the Bermuda government and other owners of these defensive works to ensure their preservation and interpretation to allow future visitors to Bermuda to enjoy the rich history of these defenses.

The authors want to thank all those who have assisted us on this project, especially Bolling Smith, Captain Stephen Card, John Singleton, Andrew Pettit, Martin Buckley, and the staff of the National Museum of Bermuda; their contributions are gratefully acknowledged. Any remaining errors are solely the responsibility of the authors. We would also like to offer special thanks to Nikolai Bogdanovic and Marcus Cowper at Ilios Publishing for efforts in creating the Fortress series and for editing this Osprey book.

The purpose of this book is to encourage readers to visit these sites to discover for themselves the tangible remains of Bermuda's coastal fortifications. Given the format of Osprey's Fortress Series, this book can only be an introductory work that gives a general understanding of Bermuda's fortifications, which stretch over almost 400 years. It does not explain the entire historical or technical development in the island's military defenses, especially the naval or air defenses. We hope this book will make clearer to readers what they will see, while explaining what is no longer there to be seen.

Terrance McGovern   Dr Edward C. Harris
1700 Oak Lane   148 Somerset Road
McLean VA 22101   Sandys Parish MA06
USA   Bermuda
tcmcgovern@att.net   scaurbda@me.com

ABOUT THE ARTIST

Adam Hook studied graphic design, and began his work as an illustrator in 1983. He specializes in detailed historical reconstructions, and has illustrated Osprey titles on subjects as diverse as the Aztecs, the Ancient Greeks, Roman battle tactics, several 19th-century American subjects, the modern Chinese Army, and a number of books in the Fortress series. His work features in exhibitions and publications throughout the world.

ARTIST'S NOTE

Readers may care to note that the original paintings from which the color plates in this book were prepared are available for private sale. All reproduction copyright whatsoever is retained by the Publishers. All enquiries should be addressed to:

Scorpio, 158 Mill Road, Hailsham, East Sussex BN27 2SH, UK

The Publishers regret that they can enter into no correspondence upon this matter.

COAST DEFENSE STUDY GROUP (CDSG)

The CDSG is a non-profit corporation formed to promote the study of coast defenses and fortifications (primarily but not exclusively those of the USA), their history, architecture, technology, and strategic and tactical employment. Membership in the CDSG includes four issues of the organization's two quarterly publications, the *Coast Defense Journal* and the *CDSG Newsletter*, attendance at the CDSG's annual conference, and special tours. The CDSG Fund makes grants to organizations for preservations and interpretation of historic coast defenses. For more information about the CDSG please visit www.cdsg.org or to join the CDSG write to Quentin Schillare, 24624 W. 96th Street, Lenexa, KS 66227-7285 USA.

FORTRESS STUDY GROUP (FSG)

The FSG was formed to provide an opportunity for those interested in fortifications and military architecture to meet, get to know one another, and publish their work. The group publishes an annual peer-reviewed journal entitled *FORT*, which contains articles on fortifications throughout the world, and *Casemate*, a newsletter published three times a year. Annual conferences and lecture days are held in the UK in order to disseminate new research on the subject. Tours of fortifications outside the UK are also organized, often with access to sites not open to the public, in cooperation with other similar groups and local councils. The group also offers small grants for the publication of works on fortification and castles, town defenses, and artillery fortifications in Britain and Ireland. For more information about the FSG, please visit www.fsgfort.com or to join the FSG contact at ask@fsgfort.com.

CONTENTS

INTRODUCTION   4

CHRONOLOGY   7

THE COLONIAL PERIOD, 1612–1783   10
Design and development

Tour of the sites and features

Garrison life

Operational history, 1612–1783

THE IMPERIAL PERIOD, 1784–1898   18
Design and development

Tour of the sites and features

The defenses of the Bermuda Dockyard

Garrison life

Operational history, 1784–1898

THE 20TH CENTURY, 1899–1995   41
Design and development

Tour of the sites and features

Garrison life

Operational history, 1899–1995

AFTERMATH, 1995–PRESENT   57

VISITING THE SITES TODAY   58

RECOMMENDED READING   60

APPENDIX: BERMUDA'S FORTS, BATTERIES, AND MILITARY RESERVATIONS   61

INDEX   64

DEFENSES OF BERMUDA 1612–1995

INTRODUCTION

Bermuda has played an important military role between America and Europe for almost 400 years due to its location in the Western North Atlantic some 635 miles off the Carolinas halfway between Halifax and Jamaica. Bermuda was a key naval base for the Royal Navy after the War of Independence in 1783, and ultimately as allies with the United States. Defending its coastline (64 miles) and ports has been vital, resulting in the construction of over 90 forts and batteries, even though its total land mass is only 20.6 square miles. This concentration of fortifications (4.4 forts per square mile), British possession, and its small size led to Bermuda gaining the informal title of the "Gibraltar of the West."

"Mount Bermuda" rises about 15,000ft from the Atlantic seabed, with its last eruptions occurring some 30 million years ago. While the top of this seamount would have been exposed during the Ice Ages, when the sea level dropped upwards of 600ft, at present volcanic rock has not been found any higher than 100ft below sea level. The limestone cap on that volcanic base rises no more than 270ft above the sea, and is a product of a coral archipelago

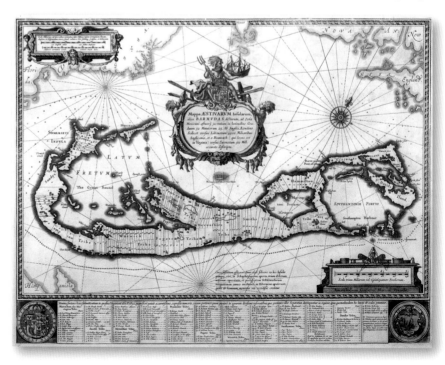

Considered one of the masterpieces of 17th-century cartography of the Americas, the Willem Blaeu map of the 1630s records how the Island was divided into shares for the investors of the Bermuda Company of London. Some of the first fortifications are noted on the map. (NMB Collections)

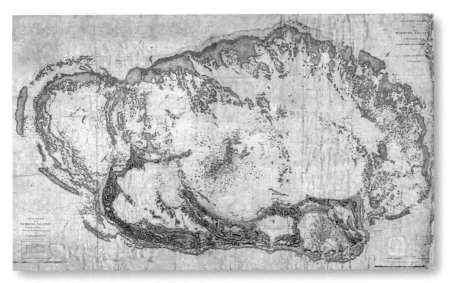

that formed on its dormant top. All the rock above sea level at Bermuda is Aeolian limestone (calcium carbonate) of varying age and hardness. It was brought into being by the creation of sand dunes, and was formed about 1.6 million to 10,000 years before the present era. Bermuda in those times would have been about ten times its present size, forming a platform of several hundred square miles upon which sand dunes could be formed. Over time, the dunes were solidified by the action of rainwater on the calcium in the sand, creating the limestone which would form the key building material for Bermuda's defenses.

At the same time, being a coral atoll, there is a geological tendency to have lagoons (harbors) created behind the protection of the line of reef fronting the open sea, unlike many volcanic islands, which tend to have few natural harbors. Bermuda's extensive coral reefs, primarily to the north, east, and west, extend up to 8 miles offshore, forming a natural defense, which has served the island well. The only channel for ships into the harbors and inner anchorages through these reefs is at the eastern end of the island. Therefore, until the beginning of the 19th century, the principal harbors were at the Town of St George and the nearby Castle Harbour, as were the military defenses and garrisons. The "Narrows Channel" (originally "Hurd's Deep") was discovered in the 1790s by a hydrographer of the Royal Navy, and since that time its presence has dictated the military development of Bermuda. This channel allowed the maritime use of Grassy Bay, the Great Sound, and Hamilton Harbour, as well as the establishment of the Royal Naval Dockyard at Ireland Island at the west end of Bermuda.

Although usually referred to in the singular, the territory consists of 181 islands. The largest island is Main Island, sometimes called Bermuda. Four of the larger islands are connected by bridges and are the populated islands. Compiling a list of the islands is often complicated, as many have more than one name (as does the entire archipelago, which has also been known historically as La Garza, the Isle of Devils, and the Somers Isles). Despite the small land mass, many place names are repeated on Bermuda, so those seeking out fortified places should keep this confusing nomenclature in mind.

As the second and now oldest English colony in the Americas, Bermuda's early fortifications focussed primarily on defending the English colonists

With HMS *Challenger* alongside the Royal Naval Dockyard in 1872, the adjacent Floating Dock, installed in 1869, is a symbol of the importance of Bermuda for British military and strategic interests in the Western North Atlantic Ocean and Caribbean Sea. (NMB Collections)

against the threat of attack from the Spanish, Dutch, and French, as well as pirates. These forts were simple works carved from the island's natural limestone, mounting naval cannon, primarily in Castle Harbour, and on Paget and St George's Islands, to deny entry of ships to these natural harbors. Bermuda's military importance increased tremendously following American independence in 1783, as the British military was forced to relocate its bases from the American mainland to Bermuda. The Royal Navy moved its naval operations for its North America & West Indies Station to Bermuda and developed its only dockyard between the Canadian Maritimes and the West Indies. The blockade of the southern US Atlantic Seaboard, as well as the sack of Washington, DC during the War of 1812 was orchestrated from the Admiralty House in Bermuda. With the buildup of the Royal Naval establishment in the first decades of the 19th century, many military fortifications were constructed and the numbers of regular infantry, artillery, and support units that composed the British Army garrison were steadily increased. The need to protect the large naval dockyard on Ireland Island resulted in over a century of fortification construction throughout the islands of Bermuda. These defenses were professionally built using current European standards with land defenses (ditches, bastions, batardeaux, caponiers, ravelins, etc.). By the end of this period technology had advanced, and the replacement of wooden sailing warships by steel steam-powered warships and the advent of large Rifled Muzzle Loader (RML) cannon required the reconstruction of Bermuda's primary forts and enlargement of its naval dockyard.

The 20th century ushered in another round of new defenses, as the great advances in military technology rendered much of the existing fortifications obsolete. The defenses of this period saw the use of concrete and breech-loading cannon, while the arrival of seaplanes (and later land-based aircraft) required new facilities. Meanwhile, the British Empire and Bermuda's defenses were tested by two world wars. The strain of the second conflict led Britain to share the burden of the island's defenses with the United States. This resulted in the construction of a range of gun batteries, army bases, seaplane facilities, naval stations, and a large airfield by the United States. The impact of this airfield on Bermuda was transforming, as it played an important role in both World War 2 and the Cold War, defending the Western North Atlantic against both German and Soviet submarines. The defense of Bermuda became the sole responsibility of the US when the last regular British Army units were withdrawn after the Royal Naval Dockyard downsized in the 1950s. With the end of the Cold War, the military importance of Bermuda declined to the point where the last British and American forces departed in 1995. The loss of its military role as an outpost for two empires (Britain and United States) had great economic impact on Bermuda, but these military defenses also provided salvation as the airfield allowed for the rise of both tourism and the insurance/banking sectors which replaced this key military spending.

Today, the legacy of these defensive works remains either as disused structures or parks scattered throughout Bermuda. Every year brings tourists to Bermuda, where they discover the remains of those extensive fortification efforts, whether it is a large stone and mortar multi-story structure surrounded by a dry ditch, or an odd-shaped, concrete structure covered with thick vegetation and surrounded by worn fences sporting weathered warning signs. Visitors are curious about the nature of these structures. Some of the questions they ask are: What are these structures? Why are they here? When were they built? These visitors turn to Bermudians for answers, but most have little information to offer these visitors. This book hopes to serve as a good source to answer those questions for both tourists and residents by providing an overview of design, primary features, and operational history of Bermuda's fortifications from the settlement of the island in 1612 to the closure of the last defense base in 1995, as well as what has happened to these fortifications since that time and which are the best defenses to visit.

CHRONOLOGY

1505	Spanish sea captain Juan de Bermúdez discovers the uninhabited Bermudas Islands.
1609	English ship *Sea Venture*, commanded by Admiral Sir George Somers, sailing for Virginia, is caught in a storm and founders on reefs off Bermuda; the crew and passengers survive.
1612	The Virginia Company sends 60 settlers to Bermuda; they establish St George as capital. The island is sold to the Bermuda Company in 1615; Paget Fort, the first Bermuda fort, is constructed to defend the channel to St George's Harbour.
1613	Richard Norwood arrives on the island. He surveys it in 1616–17 and divides it into nine parishes.
1614	Forts are constructed on Castle Island to defend Castle Harbour.
1616	Slaves are brought to Bermuda.
1620	The first Bermuda Parliament convenes at St Peter's Church. In 1621, the State House is built as its first home.
1684	British government takes control from the Bermuda Company, which is dissolved.
1701	The first British army troops are stationed on Bermuda; the militia remains Bermuda's primary defense force.
1775	American War of Independence; the Continental Congress embargoes trade with Britain and its colonies. Bermuda receives exemption in exchange for gunpowder stored at St George.
1783	The Treaty of Paris is signed between Britain and the United States, ending the American War of Independence. Britain recognizes the United States as an independent nation and loses the East Coast ports.

1790	The Royal Navy charts the channel into the inner harbors of the island.
1793	Regular Royal Army units are stationed on Bermuda on a continuing basis until 1957.
1795	The Royal Navy establishes a base at Convict Bay, St George.
1809	Britain begins to build the Royal Naval Dockyard to replace American ports lost in the War of Independence. The British plan is to transform Bermuda into a heavily fortified base, the "Gibraltar of the West."
1814	Forty-two warships leave Bermuda to attack Washington and Baltimore during the War of 1812.
1815	The capital is moved from St George's to Hamilton.
1834	Slavery is abolished in the British dominions worldwide.
1844	Gibb's Hill Lighthouse is built.
1855	Prospect Camp is established near the city of Hamilton as the principal infantry garrison, while the Royal Artillery remains at the camp at St George's.
1861	US Civil War begins and Bermudians make fortunes shipping supplies and munitions to the Confederacy.
1869	Warwick Camp is established as the British Army's rifle range. The first floating dock, "Bermuda," arrives at the Royal Naval Dockyard.
1871	A causeway is built between St George's Island and the mainland of Bermuda.
1883	Princess Louise, daughter of Queen Victoria, comes to Bermuda. Her visit helps to promote the island as a tourist destination.
1902	New Admiralty Floating Dock No. 1 (AFD1) is installed at an extension of the Royal Naval Dockyard.
1908	The Bermuda Electric Light, Power & Traction Company (now BELCO) begins supplying electricity.
1914	World War 1 begins; Bermuda sends troops to the Western Front: 80 men are lost in the conflict.
1918	The US Navy establishes a temporary support base on Agar's Island towards the end of World War 1.
1920	Coast artillery batteries reduced to a 6in. examination battery at St David's Battery
1931	The Bermuda Railway opens, from St George's to Somerset in Sandys Parish.
1937	Imperial Airways (later British Airways) and Pan American Airways begin a joint service from the US to Bermuda.
1939	World War 2 begins. A new 6in. Rifle Breech-Loader (RBL) battery of two guns is built at Warwick Camp—the last British artillery emplacement. The RAF opens seaplane bases on Darrell's Island and Boaz Island.
1940	The British government closes the Hamilton Princess Hotel to tourists and uses it as an intelligence center until the end of World War 2. Mail between the US and Europe is intercepted and analyzed there.
1941	The United States leases a large part of the island for 99 years. US Naval Operating Bases are constructed on Tucker's

	and Morgan's Islands in the Great Sound to support naval seaplanes; the US Army establishes Fort Bell and begins construction of airfield and coastal defenses on Bermuda; US Coast Artillery units arrive on Bermuda to man coast and antiaircraft artillery.
1942	A US Navy submarine base is opened on Ordnance Island, St George. US Army arrives in Bermuda to provide a mobile defense force.
1945	World War 2 ends.
1946	Fort Bell closes and is transferred to the Army Air Forces as Kindley Field. The first commercial airline service starts to Kindley Field.
1947	Bermuda's first insurance company, American International Group (AIG), is formed.
1948	The Bermuda Railway is discontinued and sold to British Guiana.
1951	The Royal Navy downsizes the Royal Naval Dockyard and sells it to the Bermuda government.
1953	The last British coast artillery battery (at St David's Head) is abandoned.
1954	The US Navy establishes a SOSUS listening post at Tudor Hill to track Soviet submarines.
1955	US Air Force air-refueling squadron is based at Kindley Field.
1957	The British Army is withdrawn and the garrison establishment is closed.
1959	A NASA tracking station is constructed on Cooper Island.
1963	The Royal Canadian Navy establishes a radio facility at Daniel's Head.
1965	The Royal Bermuda Regiment is formed from the Bermuda Militia Artillery and Bermuda Volunteer Rifle Corps.
1968	A new constitution is introduced and two-party government established; first general elections.
1970	US Navy assumes responsibility for the Kindley Air Force Base, renamed NAS Bermuda, while the former Naval Air Station at Morgan's Point becomes the NAS Annex.
1975	Queen Elizabeth II visits Bermuda and opens the Bermuda Maritime Museum (now the National Museum of Bermuda).
1982	The West End Development Corporation (WEDCO) is formed to manage the former Dockyard.
1995	The US Navy closes its bases; the Royal Navy closes HMS Malabar station.
2000	UNESCO World Heritage status is granted to the Town of St George's and associated fortifications.
2002	Bermuda's legislators enact the United States Bases (Termination of Agreement) Act.
2009	Bermuda celebrates the 400th anniversary of settlement and is visited by Her Majesty Queen Elizabeth II.
2013	The National Museum of Bermuda takes over all of the 16 acres of surviving fortifications of the old Royal Navy Dockyard at the west end of the island.

THE COLONIAL PERIOD, 1612–1783

The need to defend Bermuda began on July 11, 1612, with the arrival of the first wave of permanent English settlers on the *Plough*, with some 50-odd souls and the first governor, Richard Moore, representing the Virginia Company. This event is not as famous as the discovery of Bermuda by Juan de Bermúdez in 1505, while sailing back to Spain from a provisioning voyage to Hispaniola, nor the foundered *Sea Venture*, under the leadership of Admiral Sir George Somers, on a reef of the eastern end of Bermuda on July 28, 1609. Soon the settlers commenced construction of St George's, which would become the oldest continuously inhabited English town in the New World. In the first decade of settlement, 11 defensive works would be constructed to guard the island of St George and the access to Castle Harbour. Governor Moore began the defense of the eastern coast by choosing a location for the first fort constructed on Bermuda on Paget Island on the north side of the channel that leads into St George's Harbour.

Design and development

The early Bermudian forts were designed and constructed by the settlers themselves, financed by the Virginia Company (later the Bermuda Company). Most were carved out of the local limestone, with less than a dozen gun platforms behind a parapet pierced with embrasures that could mount a collection of smoothbore cannon on naval carriages. They were sited to fire on ships trying to enter channels into the harbors, around which the settlements were clustered. Stone walls enclosed the batteries to defend against land attack. The larger forts of this period also had keeps, towers, and small bastions to enhance their defense against land attacks. Within the walls of these forts, structures were built to support key functions: magazines for gunpowder, cookhouses and storerooms for feeding the fort's defenders, and catchments and cisterns for the vital water supply. The manpower to operate these forts was drawn from the settlers in the form of a local militia (the same workforce that was used to construct them).

The development of the colony of Bermuda would drive the need to build fortifications to defend the settlement from possible attacks by Spanish, Dutch, or French forces, as well as pirates. None of the other American colonial works compare well with the early Bermuda situation. There were no threats from indigenous inhabitants, as there were none. For whatever reason, there were no bastioned works on the island until the Dockyard defenses were erected in the 1820s. Instead, the Bermuda forts seem to return in part to an earlier era, that of the coastal defenses of England under Henry VIII. The towers and rounded parapets at Devonshire Redoubt and Warwick Castle, along with the crenellated walls and rounded bastions at Southampton Fort, can be related generally to the castles at Deal and Sandgate in Kent, UK. None of the four large forts of this period, namely, Paget, Smith's, Southampton, and the King's Castle, were typical angular bastioned works. Instead, each had a semicircular gun platform adapted to the site, with the exception of the King's Castle, where the platform follows the irregular natural limits of the site. These bulwarks stand free and clear with no ditches or earthen ramparts and outworks. They are largely offensive works, designed to pound the enemy's ships with as much iron as they could bring to bear in a limited context.

The Colonial Period, 1612–1783

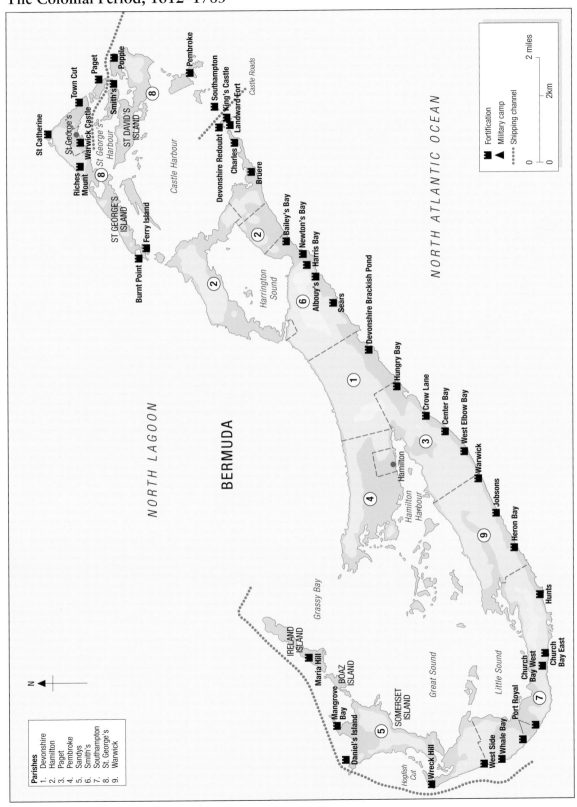

Parishes
1. Devonshire
2. Hamilton
3. Paget
4. Pembroke
5. Sandys
6. Smith's
7. Southampton
8. St. George's
9. Warwick

Fortification
Military camp
Shipping channel

0   2 miles
0   2km

NORTH ATLANTIC OCEAN

NORTH LAGOON

BERMUDA

N

St Catherine
Riches Mount
St George's
Warwick Castle
Smith's
Town Cut
Paget
Popple
Pembroke
Southampton
King's Castle
Landward Fort
Devonshire Redoubt
Charles
Bruere
Castle Roads
St George's Harbour
ST DAVID'S ISLAND
ST GEORGE'S ISLAND
Castle Harbour
Ferry Island
Burnt Point
Bailey's Bay
Newton's Bay
Harris Bay
Albouy's
Sears
Harrington Sound
Devonshire Brackish Pond
Hungry Bay
Crow Lane
Center Bay
West Elbow Bay
Warwick
Jobsons
Heron Bay
Hunts
Hamilton
Hamilton Harbour
Great Sound
Little Sound
Grassy Bay
IRELAND ISLAND
BOAZ ISLAND
Maria Hill
Mangrove Bay
Daniel's Island
SOMERSET ISLAND
Wreck Hill
West Side
Whale Bay
Port Royal
Church Bay West
Church Bay East
Hogfish Cut

11

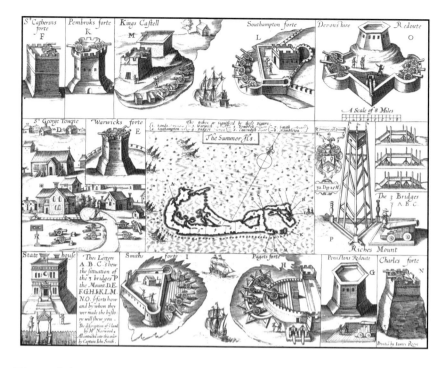

Published in 1624 by Captain John Smith (of Jamestown and Pocahontas fame), these sketches show the first ten masonry fortifications at Bermuda, constructed in the first decade of settlement (1612–22), the earliest English stone forts in the Americas. (NMB Collections)

Tour of the sites and features

Over the years these forts were in service, they were modified due to changes in colony leadership, impact of storms, developments in military technology, and the financial and manpower resources available, so we need to view each fort as a work in progress with ever-changing characteristics. By 1621, **Paget Fort** (Bermuda's first fort) was a D-shaped bastion mounting five guns that fired through embrasures onto the channel to St George's Harbour. On the opposite side was **Smith's Fort**, constructed on Governor's Island in 1613. The main armament of this fort was housed in a D-shaped battery containing embrasures for six cannon. To the rear of the water battery stood a square redoubt, the curtains of which were pierced with loopholes for muskets.

Once the primary channel to St George's Harbour was defended, Governor Moore turned to building a series of small towers to provide protection from enemy landing parties at the sites most favorable for such events. Four were along the coast (Charles, Pembroke, Peniston's, and St Catherine's forts) and a fifth (Warwick Castle) was inland and just to the north of the Town of St George. Summarized below is what we know about these towers.

Warwick Castle was apparently a hexagonal tower mounting several guns on its roof, or first-story platform, begun in the late summer of 1613 by Governor Moore. Warwick Castle may have been located on the hill now occupied by the Western Redoubt.

St Catherine's Fort was over the rise to the north, a short distance from Warwick Castle, on the northernmost tip of Bermuda, by the beach where the shipwrecked mariners from the *Sea Venture* landed in July 1609. In it were two pieces of ordnance.

Peniston's Redoubt was between St Catherine's Fort to the north and Paget Fort to the south. The coastline is broken by a little island with two small channels separating it from St George's and Paget islands. To cover these channels against boat traffic, Governor Moore erected a tower, later called Peniston's Redoubt, towards the northern end of Paget Island.

Pembroke Fort served a function similar to that of Peniston's Redoubt but a mile or so to the south. Built by Governor Moore on the seaward promontory of Cooper's Island, it covered a boat channel into Castle Harbour between Cooper's and Nonsuch islands and flanked the rear of the later Southampton Fort on the island just south of Nonsuch.

Charles Fort was south of Pembroke Fort, separated by major defensive works on Southampton and Castle islands. Charles Fort, like Pembroke, was in effect the outworks of the fortifications on those islands which flanked the channel into Castle Harbour. The best evidence we have for the design of Charles Fort shows a small, rectangular, single-story work, mounting two guns, which fired through embrasures.

By 1619, the entry to St George's Harbour had been covered effectively by Paget and Smith's forts. Governor Moore, however, was also intent upon the protection of the channel into what was originally called Southampton (later Castle) Harbour, a few miles to the south. The channels for both harbors led directly to the open sea, for the reefs on this part of the coast extend but a few hundred yards from shore.

By the 1680s, there were three forts on Castle Island, which forms part of the eastern perimeter of Castle Harbour and flanks the channel into it from the open sea. This channel, Castle Roads, has direct access to the ocean, unlike the more tortuous St George's Channel, where ships often had to be warped through, due to its change of direction and shallowness. Castle Harbour was commodious and provided good anchorage, except for the occasional gale from the northwest. It was the premier harbor in the early days of the settlement of Bermuda.

The term "King's Castle" later became a generic phrase for the forts on Castle Island. The one fronting the sea was known as the **King's Castle**. By mid-1621, the King's Castle had probably assumed the shape that one can see today. It had a lower platform for at least seven guns, which was overlooked by five cannons on the roof of a small rectangular tower in the rear. A few hundred feet to the rear of the King's Castle, the ground rises slightly to the highest point on Castle Island. It was here that Governor Moore erected a redoubt in timber, designated **Moore's Fort**. Nothing is known of its design, as it burned down in 1619 and was replaced by a small defensive tower on a pillar of bedrock, overlooking a three-part platform mounting seven guns, and renamed **Devonshire Redoubt**. The central salient of the platform is an angular, rather than circular, bastion, as were those to its left and right. The platform, which plays into the harbor, is of three parts, each a curved parapet with embrasures cut out of the bedrock.

Constructed in the later Colonial period was **Landward Fort** at the southwestern tip of Castle Island, a small redoubt still standing and fronting toward Tucker's Town. This work consisted of a lower battery of three

Archaeological excavations in the 1990s revealed the remains of the towers of Smith's Fort (built 1613), which were slighted and then buried under the new work constructed by Major Andrew Durnford, RE (Royal Engineers), in the 1790s, with embrasures for four cannon. (NMB Collections)

guns, two facing the mainland, the third firing into the bay towards Charles Island. Westward and above the battery, a curving rampart for guns firing over the parapet connected the battery with a small masonry building. To the east, the battery was linked to a curtain wall running along the southern side of Castle Island and ending at a gateway and barracks near the King's Castle.

Completing the defense of Castle Roads was **Southampton Fort** of 1621. This work had a semicircular parapet fronting Castle Roads, with five guns en barbette. To the rear was a raised courtyard with a rectangular building, and beyond that two crenellated curtains with three half-circular bastions. Fortuitously overlooked, along with the forts on Castle Island, by the inexorable march of technology and saved from modern depredations by its remote location, Southampton Fort and the works on Castle Island are by a century or more the finest standing defense works of the early English colonization of the New World.

Thus, by the end of the term of the first governor, Richard Moore, nine defensive works had been erected or begun, not counting the signal station at Moore's Mount. This number increased to 11 (mounting 45 guns) during Governor Butler's tenure, for he built two new works, Southampton Fort and Devonshire Redoubt. A listing of these forts is provided in the Appendix.

Garrison life

Manning the defenses of Bermuda was a part-time affair during the Colonial period. The governor would require the settlers to provide their services both to maintain the forts and to man them during times of possible attack, as well as serving as infantry in case of enemy landings. As a result, most defensive positions usually remained unmanned, limiting the need to build extensive barracks and cookhouses. Training of the settlers as infantry or artillerymen was limited, yet most settlers of the day knew how to use the weapons of the period, and use of cannons on land was very similar to that aboard sailing vessels.

When the Bermuda Company was dissolved in 1684, the British government took control of Bermuda. The first Crown-appointed governor, Sir Robert Robinson, found the state of defenses less than satisfactory, so he raised a militia of 780 men, with provisions made to arm those men without weapons of their own with the Militia Act of 1687. A standing watch was raised to patrol through the parishes, with three "well-armed" footmen and a horseman in each parish on each night. In 1691, a further Militia Act required every man, free or enslaved, between the ages of 15 and 60 to "appear at every exercise and muster and provide himself with sword and musket. Slave owners were responsible to provide weapons to their slaves."

A **SOUTHAMPTON FORT, 1625**

Castle Harbour was the principal anchorage in the first few decades after the settlement of Bermuda in 1612. Here a ship is about to transit the Castle Roads channel into the harbor, with the forts of Castle Island in the right background. Those defense works were flanked to the east of the channel by Southampton Fort, built by Governor Nathaniel Butler in 1621. In this view, the Bermuda militia are manning its six cannons and retrieving gunpowder from its underground magazine in case the vessel is hostile. While the front of the fort is composed for modern artillery of the day, the rear, with its rounded bastions, crenellated curtains, and gatehouse keep is a throw-back to a medieval castle. Most of Southampton Fort is still extant, making it one of the oldest surviving British works in the Americas.

Excavated in the 1990s, the King's Castle of 1612 was the citadel of the first defenses of Bermuda. Located on the seaward point of Castle Island, it defended the entrance to Castle Harbour, which was the principal anchorage of the island after the harbor at the Town of St George's. (John Singleton, 2016)

King's Castle now received a guard of four men, under a lieutenant. Two men were posted at Paget's Fort, and a lookout was regularly stationed at Moore's Mount, the highest point in St George's.

In 1702, Britain entered the War of the Spanish Succession against France. The previous year, with war looming, a company of regular infantry was sent to Bermuda and made an "independent company" (the first regular army deployment to the colony). With the onset of the war, the militia was strengthened. Six hundred men were armed and trained with lances. Despite the deployment of a regular company, the island's defenses were then completely neglected by the British government as the war with France dragged on until 1713. War with Spain was opened in 1715, and still no military supplies were dispatched to Bermuda until 1728.

In 1741, local militia, along with two Bermudian sloops, responded to a Spanish raid on Southampton Parish, but the Spaniards had retreated before the militia arrived. In 1758, after the start of the Seven Years' War, a troop of horse and a regiment of foot of nine companies were formed; each of the nine parishes was to provide a company under the command of a captain, a lieutenant, and an ensign. The end of war in 1763 led to the withdrawal of the Independent company, replaced by a detached company of the 9th Regiment of Foot, from Florida. In 1768, this company was returned to Florida, leaving Bermuda without a regular garrison. Except for a period during the American War of Independence, the colony's military defense was left, thenceforth, to its own militias until 1793.

Bermuda's defense during this period was also through ships, as Bermuda's livelihood was based on the sea. A third of her able men were always afloat, and most of those ashore were engaged in some maritime business, especially shipbuilding. Bermuda sloops, light, stiff, and deep-hulled in construction, were about the fastest things afloat. In an era of slow-moving, square-rigged ships, the sloop's ability to point high into the wind was an enormous advantage to those wanting to move quickly. Privateers, who relied on speed and audacity for success, loved them and these ships were available to defend Bermuda.

Operational history, 1612–1783

Bermuda's fortifications were a company matter; until the American War of Independence went against the British, the Crown had little military interest

Castle Island is dominated by the Devonshire Redoubt (1621), which is sited on the highest point of the island. It was substantially added to by Major Andrew Durnford in the earlier part of the period between the Treaty of Paris in 1783 and the start of the Royal Naval Dockyard in 1809, and thus marks the transition from Colonial to Imperial defense works at Bermuda. Also defending the anchorage of Castle Harbour are King's Castle (1612) on the right and Landward Fort (1630) on the left, in this photo taken in the 1980s. (NMB Collections)

in Bermuda. The first Bermuda forts were almost a family affair, put together with little expertise and much hard work by the settlers, who numbered fewer than a thousand souls in the first decade of the colony with limited funding from the Bermuda Company. The design of the forts is dissimilar to developments in continental America and represents the beginning of the coastal defense of the British Empire.

Burnt Point Fort on the northwestern point of St George's Island is typical of the small coastal batteries that were several dozen in number. They were erected primarily on the south coast of Bermuda in the 1600s to guard the beaches and other enemy landing places. This photo was taken in the 1980s. (NMB Collections)

Defenses constructed on Bermuda after the end of the first decade and before the end of the American War of Independence reflect the growing economic development of Bermuda over those 150 years. During this time, the Spanish continued as the foremost enemy, with the French not far behind. A thousand miles from the Bahamas and further still to the other British West Indies possessions, Bermuda was not involved in the land skirmishes and sea battles of that area. As long as "sugar was king," the emphasis on British military fortifications in the Americas was in the West Indies, and magnificent works such as Brimstone Hill Fort in St Kitts were not duplicated in Bermuda. Rather, the settlers, although under the British government upon the dissolution of the Bermuda Company in 1684, continued to build their own small and primitive fortifications throughout the islands. As the number of colonists continued to grow, Bermuda was subdivided into "tribes" or "parishes" to allow cultivation to spread outward from St George's Island to all of the "Greater Bermuda" islands. The general defense trend is obvious: after coping with the exigencies of protecting the new town and settlement at the eastern end of St George's Island, the colonists on Bermuda undertook to fortify their own backyards. Small redoubts of varying shapes and dimensions were erected on most of the landing places afforded by the beaches of the South Shore as well as possible landing areas on the west coast of Bermuda.

Originally a work of the 1620s, Davers Fort was eventually (erroneously) named "Gate's Fort," and in its present state marks the rebuilding of the structure in the two decades immediately following the end of the American War of Independence (1783). The photo was taken in 2016. (John Singleton)

In the successive decades, but possibly starting as early as 1617, not fewer than 27 batteries were built on the south and west coasts. At various dates, some undetermined but all before 1783, at least nine other redoubts were built on St George's Island, along with the Paget Fascine Battery on Paget Island, Fort Popple on St David's Island, and Landward Fort on Castle Island. This gives a total of about 50 colonial forts in Bermuda at the turn of the military epoch in 1783 (see the Appendix for a listing of these forts) mounting a total of 145 pieces of ordnance after 171 years of fort-building and armament by the Bermudians themselves at the end of the American War of Independence. These defenses served their purpose well; the sole recorded attacks resulted in only two cannon shots in 1614—the only shots ever fired in anger.

THE IMPERIAL PERIOD, 1784–1898

In 1775, the peace of the British overseas possessions in North America was shattered when Massachusetts colonists took up arms against British troops. All 13 colonies on the eastern seaboard were eventually involved in this civil war, which led to independence from Britain in 1783. The Bermudians used both sides to their advantage in the conflict and went as far as to steal gunpowder from the magazine at St George's to sell to and barter with the Americans. They did remain essentially loyal to the Crown. The American War of Independence was won in part because of a temporary naval supremacy by the French Navy, a fact not lost on the British forces. As the war ended, the British military looked to Bermuda as a possible replacement for the lost naval bases of the eastern seaboard of the new United States of America. The British government sent several officers of the Corps of Royal Engineers (RE), the "purveyors of technology to the empire," to Bermuda to start this transformation, foremost of whom was Andrew Durnford, RE. However, 25 years would pass before work began on Bermuda's Royal Naval Dockyard. He was extremely active during his ten-year posting as he altered, repaired, or built anew a number of Bermuda's East End fortifications. In total, seven existing forts were extensively repaired and three either new or virtually new works were constructed.

This brings the number of forts at Bermuda by 1809 to 62 installations and 135 guns (see the Appendix for a listing of these forts.)

Design and development

At the end of the American War of Independence, the Royal Navy lost its bases on the eastern seaboard of the United States. The base at Halifax became a major factor in the revised strategic plan for the Western North Atlantic. To the south, Antigua, Jamaica, and St Lucia contributed to holding the southern sector of the new defensive line. Halfway between Canada and the West Indies stood Bermuda, which became the object of British military interest after 1783 and the new center of that line. This caused the British to move Bermuda in significance from one of its many colonies to an important part of the worldwide imperial defense system. The Crown now moved military manpower and financial resources to Bermuda. As a first step, Royal Engineers were sent to survey and renovate the existing fortifications. At the same time, Lieutenant Thomas Hurd, a hydrographer of the Royal Navy, completed a study of the reefs and anchorages in 1797, discovering "Hurd's Channel," or the "Narrows," which allowed warships to access the protective waters of Bermuda's Northern Lagoon.

In 1795, the Admiralty approved the purchase of Ireland Island as the site for its naval base because of a "new" channel. The wheels of bureaucracy turned slowly and it was not until 1809 that work began on the new base. After the battle of Waterloo in 1814, the French threat was eliminated, but work on supporting fortifications for the Royal Naval Dockyard at the eastern end of Bermuda had already begun. The construction of the Dockyard itself was advanced greatly in 1823 by the importation of convicts from Britain, who remained the primary labor force until their removal in 1864. By the end of the American Civil War in 1865, Bermuda's defenses comprised eight entirely new fortifications. The Dockyard's fortifications stood as one of the last bastioned works ever constructed by the British; a fashionable

The Imperial Period, 1784–1898

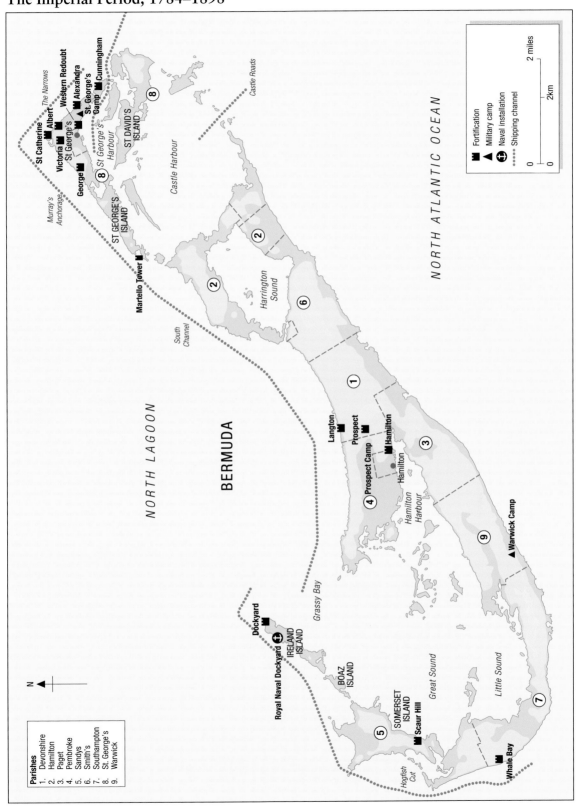

Parishes
1. Devonshire
2. Hamilton
3. Paget
4. Pembroke
5. Sandys
6. Smith's
7. Southampton
8. St. George's
9. Warwick

Fortification
Military camp
Naval installation
Shipping channel

NORTH LAGOON

BERMUDA

NORTH ATLANTIC OCEAN

Western Redoubt
Albert
St Catherine
Victoria
George
St George's
St George's Camp Cunningham
Alexandra
St George's
St George's Harbour
ST DAVID'S ISLAND
Castle Roads
Castle Harbour
The Narrows
Murray's Anchorage
ST GEORGE'S ISLAND
Martello Tower
Harrington Sound
South Channel
Langton
Prospect
Hamilton
Prospect Camp
Hamilton
Hamilton Harbour
Warwick Camp
Dockyard
Royal Naval Dockyard
IRELAND ISLAND
BOAZ ISLAND
SOMERSET ISLAND
Scaur Hill
Grassy Bay
Great Sound
Little Sound
Whale Bay
Hogfish Cut

0   2 miles
0   2km

Perhaps on a heavily overcast winter day in 1857, Gaspard le Marchant Tupper painted this image of the Dockyard's land defenses from a ship anchored in Grassy Bay. The Casemate Barracks on the hill to the left is one of the three significant buildings completed by the late 1850s, the others being the Great Eastern Storehouse with its towers, and (out of view) the Commissioner's House. The convict hulks between the barracks and the Storehouse accommodated the English and Irish prisoners who largely built the Dockyard from 1823 to 1863. (NMB Collections)

Martello Tower defended the back door of St George's Island, with six other works at the eastern end of that island and one on Paget Island. Five of the latter were constructed on the new "polygonal trace" design for fortifications, while Fort St Catherine perhaps straddles several styles. The design of Buildings Bay Battery is unclear due to the lack of records and subsequent reworking. Rather than having projecting bastions to cover the flanks and curtain walls, the polygonal forts were set within deep ditches. At the appropriate corners, reverse fire or flanking galleries for riflemen were excavated into the counterscarp, and entered by tunnels from the fort and under the floor of the ditch. These were also the last forts to be built at Bermuda for the employment of smoothbore cannon, artillery that had remained largely unchanged for over three centuries.

After the difficulties presented by the American Civil War and with major changes in weaponry and naval technology in progress, the British military in 1865 reassessed the defenses of their overseas stations. Bermuda was deemed to be the most important naval station in the Atlantic. Its central position in that ocean, within three days' steaming distance of the shores of North America, its dockyard, and capacious deepwater harbors, together with its natural capabilities for defense, contributed to render it the citadel of British naval power in the Americas. There was reason to believe that the desire of the Americans for its possession was in proportion to its value to Britain. Accordingly, the British sent Colonel Drummond Jervois, RE, Deputy Director of Fortifications, to Bermuda to inspect the existing works and make recommendations for the future.

His main interest was the Dockyard and the four forts facing the Narrows Channel. Jervois thought the Dockyard defenses were no match for the new technology. In his view, a similar situation pertained at the Narrows, where the existing batteries were all well placed, but having been constructed only to oppose wooden sailing men-of-war, they were not sufficiently powerful, either in construction or armament, to stop ironclad steam vessels armed with the powerful ordnance of the day. They were built of masonry, which could not resist the battering of the most modern heavy ordnance; the parapets were also of masonry and their guns, being nearly all en barbette, would be easily silenced by the fire of rifled ordnance. Jervois' report called for a range of improvements to be made to Bermuda's fortifications.

Fort St Catherine was to become a battery for 30 guns in two tiers, one casemated and one on the roof, to be constructed adjacent to the existing work. The parapet of the old work was to be changed to accept iron shields, which should also be applied to Buildings Bay Battery (soon to become Alexandra Battery) and Fort Cunningham. The other forts on St George's Island could be left as they were except to add some slightly bigger guns. Moving toward the Dockyard, Jervois called for a line of works to the west of the Admiral's House at Spanish Point. These were to stop an enemy from bombarding the Dockyard from that land location, as recommended in the

Defence Report of 1857, but he moved the forts to the east, to the Prospect Hill Position. Further west, his recommendations for the Hogfish Cut Channel later took shape as Whale Bay Battery. To cut off an overland approach to the Dockyard, what became Scaur Hill Fort was proposed for Somerset Island between Ely's Harbour and the Great Sound. Many of the defenses that Jervois called for were built as described in the following section.

Tour of the sites and features

Martello towers (circular masonry seacoast batteries) came into vogue in the early 19th century. In 1822, a **Martello Tower** was built at the southwestern tip of St George's Island at Ferry Point. It was set in a ditch 18ft wide, the only entry being positioned 10ft above the floor of the ditch and reached by a drawbridge, while the tower is 34ft from foundation to parapet. The Ferry Point tower has the characteristic ovoid shape with walls from 10ft 6in. to 6ft 6in. thick made from "hard-stone," being the older and more indurated form of aeolian limestone native to Bermuda. Its only gun was mounted on the roof in 1828, forming a well so that the gun could traverse a complete circle. In 1857, the gun was an 18-pdr, firing over the parapet. This tower was to prevent an enemy crossing from the main island to St George's Island, to keep up communication between them and to command the passage from St George's and Castle Harbour into the Murray's Anchorage. The Martello Tower was not altered in the RML era and went out of use toward the end of the 19th century, due in part to the rearming of Fort George in the 1870s.

Fort George was reconstructed in the 1830s on the hill where Bermuda's first signal station stood in 1622. The site had been modified in the 1790s, when Andrew Durnford added an irregular work. St George's Hill is about 1,100 yards from Retreat Hill, and 160ft high, on the western side of the town, commanding the harbor and the entrance from the ferry. St George's Hill is mainly precipitous on two sides; this work on it added to the security of Retreat Hill as it would be difficult to reduce it, and no attack could be made on the other works from this side whilst it held out.

The general plan of the fort survives today and it is possible to reconstruct the arrangement of the fort in the 1840s–50s. The Keep had two entrances via drawbridges to the north and south. It had three floors and access to two counterscarp galleries was by way of a tunnel under the ditch from the ground floor. The casemated upper floor supported the guns in the roof well above, while a middle floor served as barrack accommodation. With the exception of the roof details, the interior floors and the galleries are largely intact as built in the late 1830s. The exterior walls of the Keep and its ditch remain much the same. All traces of this work on the roof of the Keep was buried in the construction of a radio station in the 1970s, but the fort had two 24-pdrs on the roof of the Keep, while the terreplein or covered way had four 8in. guns (68-pdrs), the largest in the British arsenal at the time.

Fort George was rearmed during the RML period. The Keep seems to have been changed the least, with only the roof platforms being altered to take four 64-pdr RMLs of 58 cwt. To the north and south, the terreplein was remodeled for two 64-pdr RMLs of 58 cwt, while to the east and west, it was extensively remade for two 11in. RMLs of 25 tons. Below these guns, the terreplein was excavated for the insertion of shell and cartridge stores. Fort George was not rearmed in the breech-loading period and its massive 11in.

The only Martello Tower in Bermuda was completed in 1823. It was built of the very hard variety of local Aeolian limestone and is of the classic South Coast of England design. A replica carriage and original cannon was emplaced on its roof platform in recent times, as shown in this photo taken in the early 2000s. (NMB Collections)

RMLs are the only such guns mounted in their original positions in Bermuda.

In his report of 1823, Major Blanshard, RE, recommended several new works, the one on Retreat Hill to the rear of Fort St Catherine becoming Fort Victoria. The erection of that work became the justification for another. Located some 800 yards east of Fort George, the **Western Redoubt (Fort William)** is almost identical in plan to it, but was completed some years later. Fort George defended the landward approach from the west to the Town of St George, Murray's Anchorage to the north and covered the harbor. Western Redoubt protected the harbor and coastline to the southeast. It was finished in 1853 and is a square masonry, bombproof tower of three stories at about 138ft above sea level, built to accommodate a garrison of 75, with cistern, magazine, provision storerooms, and artillery stores. The fort was entered from the north; but for the "epaulment"(a retaining wall to protect against from direct fire), its shape would have mirrored that of Fort George. The fate of the fort as a defensive work was sealed in a report of 1869, which recommended that the Western Redoubt need not be armed, but used for storing munitions. In the late 1880s, that intention was carried out in a spectacular way when the Western Redoubt was converted into an enormous powder magazine by roofing over the ditch and the Keep.

Several hundred yards northeast of the Western Redoubt was **Fort Victoria**, which came to be the citadel of the defenses of St George's Island. Fort Victoria was begun in the late 1820s and survived until the early 1960s, when it was unfortunately degraded in the building of a hotel, though much of value and interest remains. The site was first proposed in 1823 by Major Blanshard in his report to the inspector-general of fortifications. The hexagonal fort was approved later in 1826 by the Duke of Wellington and construction began soon thereafter. The definitive description of the final version of Fort Victoria in the smoothbore period is given in the British defense report of 1857:

> Fort Victoria is about 2,191 yards from Fort Cunningham, and from its commanding position (about 52 feet above Fort Albert) in every direction may be considered the citadel of St George's with reference to either Land or Sea Attack. Its form is an irregular oblong with a ravelin to each of its two long North and South faces, it contains bombproof cover barracks for 6 Officers and 194 Men; with Tanks, Powder Magazines, provisions and Artillery Stores, & separated by a deep ditch flanked by reverse fires from an envelope, carrying on its ramparts and ravelins (again surrounded by deep ditches, covert ways, and good glacis), 18 24 Pounders, 2 18 Pounders, and 2 8 inch Mortars, the guns (except in the 2 18 Prs which are on ground platforms) all mounted on iron traversing platforms, and bearing in every direction; seawards, on the Ship Channel at a minimum distance of about 1,000 yards, up to the eastern entrance at about 2,500 yards, on part of Murray's Anchorage at about 1,800 yards; and the Naval Tanks at about 500 yards; on the town and St George's Harbour, up to its inner entrance by Fort Cunningham. With Fort Albert, which it commands at 248 yards; it commands and supports Fort Catherine at 400 yards. It also commands the Western

Redoubt at 220 yards, and the Barrack Hill and crosses its fire with that of Fort George (1,000 yards) on St George's Harbour; and it sweeps the whole tongue of land forming the eastern end of St George's Island, up to Fort Cunningham.

An apt description of a magnificent building. Fort Victoria was without a doubt the most elaborate fortification in Bermuda in the 1850s.

At Fort Victoria in the 1870s, the gun terreplein, and north ravelin were altered for RMLs. The ravelin was converted to take an 11in. RML of 25 tons. Two other 11in. RMLs of 25 tons were fitted into the modified western parapet of the terreplein. This arrangement makes it clear that the main area to be covered by Fort Victoria was Murray's Anchorage and the land approaches to Fort St Catherine and Retreat Hill. The remainder of the terreplein was made to conform with eight 64-pdr RMLs of 58 cwt.

Fort George occupies the high hill on the western flank of the Town of St George's and was last rearmed in the 1870s RML period with two 11in., 25-ton RMLs, being nos. 12 and 14 of Mark II, made at the Royal Gun Factory, Woolwich Arsenal, in 1871. The RMLs have remained in place since then, as shown in this 1995 photo. (McGovern Collection)

Fort Albert (Eastern Redoubt) is on a small hill about 300 yards east of the summit of Retreat Hill, commanding the southern approach to Fort St Catherine and capable of affording collateral assistance to the other works of the position, as well as an additional battery bearing on the ship channel that would materially strengthen that side of St George's and cooperate in the defense of the Narrows. Fort Albert was about half the size of Fort Victoria and surrounded by a ditch. Fortunately, the survey of 1857 gives an excellent description of the site in its days as a smoothbore fortification drew to a close:

> Proceeding up channel, Fort Albert stands at an elevation of about 114 feet above the level of the Sea, and is a Pentagonal Masonry Redoubt, with escarp

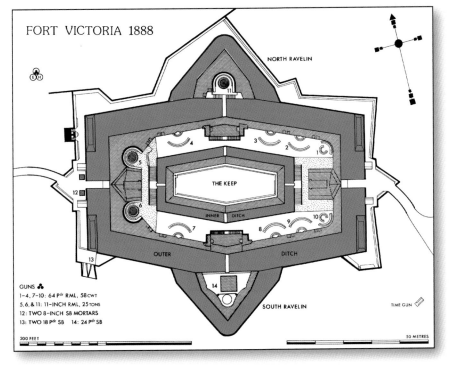

FORT VICTORIA 1888

NORTH RAVELIN

THE KEEP

INNER DITCH

OUTER DITCH

SOUTH RAVELIN

TIME GUN

GUNS ♣
1–4, 7–10: 64 P^dr RML, 58 CWT
5, 6, & 11: 11-INCH RML, 25 TONS
12: TWO 8-INCH SB MORTARS
13: TWO 18 P^dr SB   14: 24 P^dr SB

200 FEET

50 METRES

Demolished during a hotel construction in the 1970s, the Keep of Fort Victoria, constructed in the 1820s and accessed by four drawbridges, is now only preserved in plans such as this one. The gun terreplein reflects the smoothbore armament of that period, as well as the RMLs of the 1870s. (Harris Collection)

and ditch of ample height and width flanked by reverse fires, covered by a glacis, and mounting behind earthen parapets seven 32 Pounders on iron traversing platforms, bearing on the channel, and two 8 inch howitzers on ground platforms, flanking the land approach from the South East. It also mounts two 10 inch Mortars and has an Addison's furnace for heating shot. A bombproof Barrack or Keep in one of the rear Angles, with separate ditch and drawbridge will accommodate 1 Officer and 34 Men and it has a Tank and Stores in its basement.

The renovation of Fort Albert for the RML phase of armaments began in April 1865 and took 11 years to complete. In 1869, it was suggested that the guns be placed on Moncrieff disappearing carriages, but due to cost, four 10in. RMLs of 18 tons on barbette carriages were used instead. The features at the rear of the fort, namely, the Keep, the howitzer platforms, ancillary buildings, and the drawbridge remained intact. In the center of the fort, however, excavations were made several stories deep, the upper part becoming shell hoists below each gun. These connected through ammunition shafts to a new magazine complex below. In the early 1960s, the RMLs were moved to Fort St Catherine when it became a tourist attraction.

In the 1820s, **Fort St Catherine** was rebuilt as part of the defensive system to protect access to the new dockyard by covering the head of the Narrows Channel where it makes a turn before entering into Murray's Anchorage. Fort St Catherine of 1825 was thus the fourth or fifth defense work of that name, but it was not the one we see today, as it was reconstructed again in the 1840s and again in the 1890s. While no British plans remain from this time, by using reports from that period we know the fort's design was fundamentally changed and the new structure that was built in the 1830s defines the limits of the existing work to seaward. So, by 1857, the fort mounted 26 guns: three 24-pdrs on the roof of the Keep; two 24-pdr carronades flanking the main ditch from the basement of the Keep, and around the ramparts facing the sea, seven 8in. guns, twelve 32-pdrs and two 24-pdrs.

As the most powerful single fort on St George's, with 26 guns at the end of the smoothbore period and the northern guardian of the Narrows Channel, it was important that Fort St Catherine be rearmed in the RML era. Four years after his 1865 visit, Colonel Jervois made another trip to Bermuda for a further assessment of the plans to mount six guns on Moncrieff carriages. That plan was not carried out and none of the larger Moncrieff disappearing carriages were ever employed at Bermuda. By 1894, less than a decade from their obsolescence, five 10in. RMLs of 18 tons had been installed at Fort St Catherine. Two were under the concrete cover of a Haxo casemate and the

B FORT VICTORIA, 1852

Second in size only to the extensive fortifications of the western Bermuda Dockyard, Fort Victoria was the citadel of the eastern end of the Island and the largest of all the works erected in St George's Parish in the 19th century. Sadly, much of the center of the fort was demolished in the late 1960s, so this artwork represents the look of it at the apogee of the smoothbore period in the late 1850s. Gunners of the Royal Garrison Artillery are seen conducting drill on the fort's 22 cannons (mainly 24-pdrs on iron traversing carriages). Eight drawbridges connected the outer and inner features of the fort, which included the central barracks, the terreplein for the cannon and the two ditches (with counterfires) and ravelin towers. The terreplein and the south ravelin tower and some of the counterscarp of the outer ditch are still extant.

This painting dated 1857 by Gaspard le Marchant Tupper in the Fay and Geoffrey Elliott Collection shows the strategic layout of forts Albert, Victoria, and Catherine in the defenses of the Narrows Channel and the eastern flank of St George's Island. (NMB Collections)

others in large concrete and brick embrasured emplacements, which took up much space on the terreplein. Two 64-pdr RMLs were situated in the two western extremities of the fort, while a 7in. RBL stood on the northern parapet. On the southern side of the fort, a major excavation produced an area for a large magazine of five rooms, light passages, and shell and cartridge hoists.

At some point, the barrels of the big RMLs were dumped into the sea, where they lay until recently, and the carriages were cut up. So ended the development of Fort St Catherine, which began in 1612 and ran through at least seven periods of development or replacement. The site was not rearmed after the RML period, and thus ended its use as a key military site after almost three centuries.

In 1865, W. Drummond Jervois, deputy director of fortifications, made the only known reference to **Buildings Bay Battery**. His report, accurate in other respects, describes the battery at Buildings Bay, for five 68-pdrs about 30ft above the sea, with a small guardhouse, not bombproof, at the gorge. This description places the battery at the site of the later Alexandra Battery.

The coming of ironclad ships and rifled artillery did not change the strategic importance of the Narrows Channel at the east end of Bermuda, and in 1869 it could be reported that **Alexandra Battery**, formerly called

In the late 1860s, Fort St Catherine was altered to take five 10in., 18-ton RMLs and other new guns of that period. This plan shows the layout of the rebuilding and the final phase of the fort's armaments. (Harris Collection)

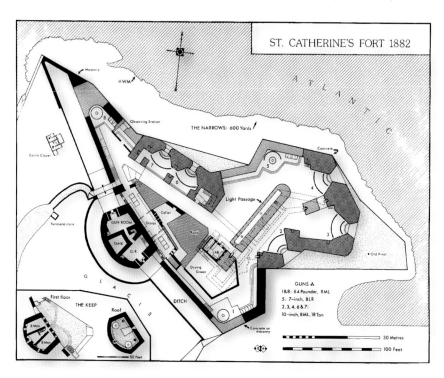

ST. CATHERINE'S FORT 1882

THE NARROWS: 600 Yards

GUNS ♣
1&8: 64 Pounder, RML
5: 7-inch, BLR
2, 3, 4, 6 & 7:
10-inch, RML, 18 Ton

30 Metres

100 Feet

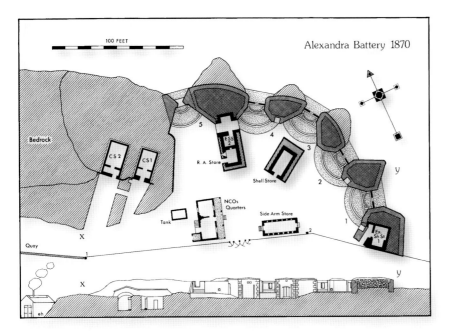

Alexandra Battery 1870

Buildings Bay Battery was rebuilt in the 1870s as the Alexandra Battery, mounting five 9in. RMLs behind armored shields. This plan shows the battery as constructed during the breech-loading era; this work was built over for two 6in. breech-loading guns, and only one emplacement can be seen today. (Harris Collection)

Buildings Bay Battery, had been prepared for five 9in. RMLs protected by iron shields. With the exception of a small barracks in connection with the gorge, and some further work in the magazines, the battery was complete. The new work was described as an arc to the east and south from the side of a small hill just east of Buildings Bay. All of the emplacements were open to the rear, with no evidence of casemates. At the turn of the century, the site was modified to take two 6in. RBLs and most of the RML works were buried in the process.

In the 1790s, Captain Andrew Durnford raised an entirely new work on the hill on the southern half of Paget Island, which he called **Upper Paget Fort**. It was a rectangular structure with a barrack attached to the north side and in 1798 mounted one 8in. howitzer, two 18-pdrs and four 12-pdrs, of which nothing remains today as this site was used for a new fort named for its designer, Captain Thomas Cunningham, RE. **Fort Cunningham** commanded the eastern entrances into St George's Harbour, the channel into Murray's Anchorage, and the anchorage in Five Fathom Hole. At terreplein level in 1823, there were ten 24-pdrs on traversing platforms, a barracks with stores below, and a casemated magazine for 300 barrels of powder. The fort was a pentagonal redoubt set in a ditch. All of Fort Cunningham above the decorative cordon of the parapet was removed in the 1870s, but the stonework below at ditch level was retained and later mostly buried. The reason for its renovation was to contain the largest RMLs ever mounted at Bermuda behind two continuous iron fronts in the "Gibraltar Shield" tradition. This new work was the most modern and heavily armed of the works constructed at Bermuda in the RML period.

The whole of the upper works were swept away and in their place arose an armored fort for nine guns. This was not to be a masonry structure with shields, such as Alexandra Battery, but a fort with an entire wrought-iron design. The cost of the iron shield and armored forts was immense, leading one exasperated British MP to stand up in Westminster and ask, "Is Fort Cunningham made of gold?"

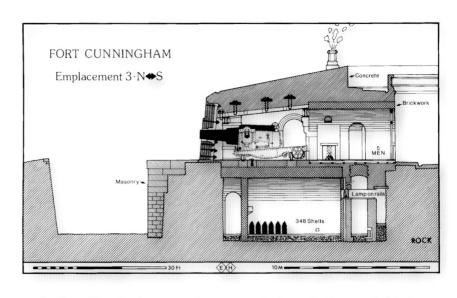

At Fort Cunningham, emplacements 1 through 7 were behind two continuous iron shields, but unlike the circular structures such as the Plymouth Breakwater Fort, these were straight fronts. Similar to the shields at Alexandra Battery, the Cunningham wrought-iron walls are almost twice as thick and substantially stronger, having interior reinforcing of teak and solid iron beams. All of the emplacements were casemated with wrought-iron plate ceilings capped with several feet of concrete. The first two emplacements (nos. 1 and 2) looked toward St David's Head and Five Fathom Hole, protecting as well the channel into St George's Harbour, between Paget and Smith's Island; here were mounted 10in. RMLs of 18 tons. Emplacements 3 and 4 were to house the largest-caliber guns ever mounted in a Bermuda fort, namely, 12.5in. RMLs of 38 tons. Emplacements 5, 6, and 7, on the same face as the 12.5in. pieces, had the same purpose, namely to cover the entrance to the Narrows Channel. They mounted 10in. RMLs of 18 tons. Facing north and covering the shoreline toward Alexandra Battery were emplacements 8 and 9, in stone and brick casemates for 9in. RMLs of 12 tons, removed apparently in the late 1880s. At the rear of the guns and the casemate, the area was used for barracks. Across the courtyard to the rear of the fort were the officers' quarters and ancillary rooms for the garrison.

In the early 1900s, the fort was converted for the last time, this time for the installation of two 6in. RBLs on the roof above emplacements 2 and 7. Below the new guns, a massive pillar of concrete was placed to carry their weight, which filled parts of the RML emplacements, including the gun ports. The RMLs from emplacements 1 to 7 were taken from their positions, lifted onto the roof over Emplacement 8, and pushed into the ditch. The guns were found in 1991 under the

backfilling of that section of the ditch, which occurred around 1905. They were in remarkably good condition; the two 38-ton guns are very rare, there being only six known examples in the world. After alterations and infilling in the late 1880s, the exposed frontage of Fort Cunningham was camouflaged by painting thick, erratic black lines on the vertical faces and on the sloping roofs, geometric red strips being the order of the day.

The defenses of the Bermuda Dockyard

The Bermuda Dockyard was established in 1809 and the yard was begun at the eastern half of Ireland Island, centered on a small cove known as Grassy Bay. Storehouses, residences, and other buildings were soon constructed in timber and soft Bermuda stone. These buildings were eventually demolished as the entire yard was rebuilt in hard Bermuda limestone in the 1840s and 1850s. The building of the Dockyard defenses took a little over 20 years from 1822 until the completion of the Right Advance in 1843. From 1823, the primary workforce comprised British convicts and local labor, including slaves, supervised by military and naval personnel. Over a 40-year period from 1823, more than 9,000 convicts were sent to the hulks at Bermuda, a quarter of whom died as a result of the conditions of service. They were employed in most aspects of the work, from "jumping" rock, to the making of ashlar blocks, and for the building itself. The working of the hardstone meant blasting and all other methods used for monumental stonework. The resulting buildings and defense works are thus splendid architectural monuments, unlike any other buildings in Bermuda.

It is difficult to give a precise schedule of the construction of the defenses of the Bermuda Dockyard. The excavation of the ditch was obviously begun in the early 1820s, while the Keep was started shortly after 1823 and was completed by the end of the decade. The Couvre Porte was probably started in 1827 and the Ravelin Tower and Land Front a short time later. The long Northwest Rampart may have been started late in the 1820s as the doorway to Bastion H on this line has a date-stone of 1835. The Right Advance appears to have been the final work, dating to the early 1840s. The following descriptive study of the Dockyard defenses is given in topographical rather than chronological order, beginning with the gateway and proceeding eastward. Notes on the armament of each structure are based on the 1857 defense report.

The Couvre Porte

The Dockyard was entered from a road on the eastern side of Ireland Island which passed over a drawbridge into the Couvre Porte, an irregular outwork surrounded by a ditch, except to the east, where it stood originally on the waters of Grassy Bay. The glacis extended from the Couvre Porte to the western side of Ireland Island, in front to the ditch of the Land Front and the other outworks. Another drawbridge to the north connected the Couvre Porte to the gate in the South Orillon. The ditch around the Couvre Porte was terminated by batardeaux on Grassy Bay and joined the Land Front ditch to the west. The western and eastern ramparts of the Couvre Porte had firing steps for musketry. In the southwest corner of this outwork a cannon covered the roadway. This salient mounted a 24-pdr in 1857. The Couvre Porte was not rearmed in the RML period and was demolished in the construction of the South Yard between 1901 and 1907.

The South Orillon

The eastern end of the Land Front formed the South Orillon, which fronted Grassy Bay and was later joined to the Short Arm Breakwater by a batardeau. It contained a casemate for three 24-pdr carronades, and on the roof were two positions, probably for 24-pdr cannon. In front, or south, of this Great Wharf Rampart was a moat open to the sea. A drawbridge connected the Short Arm with the Dockyard via an archway in the rampart. The curtain wall is all that survives above ground today as the South Orillon and the Great Wharf Rampart were destroyed in the construction of the South Yard works about 1905. There is no evidence that the South Orillon or the Great Wharf Rampart were rearmed after 1865 with RMLs.

The Ravelin Tower

The central outwork of the Land Front was the Ravelin Tower and its Counterguard. The tower was entered at first-floor level from the southern side of Casemate Barracks, through a tunnel in the Land Front, and across a bridge; another bridge joined the tower to the Counterguard. The Ravelin Tower was a casemated irregular hexagon built to hold 22 men, with a 24-pdr in each of its flanks. Four 24-pdr carronades in the casemates flanked the ditch in both directions. The Counterguard mounted one 24-pdr in its salient and had reverse fires in its counterscarp, covering the ditch of the Ravelin Tower. All evidence of the Ravelin Tower and its Counterguard was removed in the extension of the dockyard from 1901 to 1907.

The Right Advance

The last of the three outworks of the Land Front was the Right Advance. It was a structure of three tiers and contained emplacements for three cannons, entered by a tunnel under the ditch of the Land Front from the yard of Casemate Barracks. The purpose of the Right Advance was to enfilade the western shore of Ireland Island, to bear on the small boat channel from westward, and to flank the sea face of the Northwest Rampart. Neither the Right Advance nor the Ravelin Tower were rearmed in the RML period.

The Land Front

The Land Front extended across Ireland Island and in front of it was a defensive ditch; on Grassy Bay, it terminated at the South Orillon. Its eastern half-bastion above the South Orillon mounted five 24-pdrs, the upper four being terraced to match the ground. The western half-bastion of the Land Front, which ended at the Right Advance, carried three 24-pdrs and probably a 32-pdr on its westernmost emplacement. The flanks of the Land Front facing the Ravelin Tower each mounted two 24-pdr carronades, with a like number in casemates below. The hill on which the front stands is about 90ft above the sea, giving it good command of the southern part of Ireland Island. The glacis of the Land Front extended about 100 yards beyond the Ravelin Tower and was considered to be steep. In the rear of the Land Front was the bombproofed Casemate Barracks, built for 13 officers and 307 men. On the flanks of the barracks were bombproof magazines for 2,500 barrels of gunpowder.

The Northwest Rampart

Connecting the defenses of the Land Front with the Keep at the northeast point of Ireland Island was the Northwest Rampart. The terreplein of the rampart also served as the only road to the Commissioner's House and the upper grounds of the Keep, until the early 20th century, when a road was cut from the Keep yard. At the northern end of the rampart, the road passed over a rolling bridge into the Keep. On the western side of the rampart, a firing step was provided along most of its length. It was interrupted by Bastion "H" in the middle of the rampart and terminated on the northern edge of Bastion "I." The latter, next to the Land Front, was open in the rear. In the late 1850s, it mounted seven 32-pdrs on iron traversing platforms. The central work, Bastion "H," had a small moat at its gorge. It contained a casemated barrack for 22 men, water tanks, and powder magazines. On its terreplein were five 32-pdrs on iron platforms; the two in the rear could traverse to sweep the interior and basin of the Dockyard.

The Royal Naval Dockyard at Ireland Island, Bermuda, was the reason for the construction of all the British fortifications and gun batteries between 1809 and the end of British coastal defense in 1957. Its defense works now comprise the 16 acres of the National Museum of Bermuda. This photo was taken in 2014. (NMB Collections)

The Keep of the Dockyard

At the eastern end of Ireland Island was the "Keep," or citadel, of the Dockyard defenses. It was a 9-acre fort, with seven irregular bastions. The lower ground, or Keep Yard, contained the sea service stores, with two bombproof magazines for 6,540 barrels of powder, a shell store, a filling room, and a shifting house. Lighters from the Keep Pond served the fleet at anchor in Grassy Bay with munitions from these stores, or removed them thereto if a ship was under repairs in the Dockyard.

Working counter-clockwise from the moated entrance, the armament of the Keep in the late 1850s was as follows. The entrance was flanked by four 24-pdr carronades, with a 24-pdr in each salient. On the curtain approaching Bastion "A" were a 24-pdr and three 24-pdr carronades. Bastion "A" carried five 8in. shell guns, and on the curtain towards Bastion "B" were three more guns of that caliber. Bastion "B" mounted one 8in. shell gun and four 24-pdrs, with three 24-pdr carronades in casemates flanking the watergate to the Keep Pond, and the curtain to Bastion "C." At that spot, five 24-pdrs could be brought into action, supported by an additional 24-pdr in its northern curtain. Bastion "D" mounted six 24-pdrs and also had a 24-pdr in the curtain shared with Bastion "E." The latter, marking the tip of Ireland Island, had a 32-pdr and two 24-pdrs on the terreplein and four 24-pdr carronades in casemates below. These flanked the 30ft-high walls towards Bastions "D" and "F." Another 32-pdr was mounted in the flank towards Bastion "F," which was armed with four 24-pdrs and a 32-pdr in its salient. The curtain between bastions "F" and "G" held five 8in. shell guns, and on its southern flank were two 24-pdrs on ground platforms. Bastion "G" mounted six 32-pdrs, and on the far side of the drawbridge to the Northwest Rampart was a 24-pdr carronade in an embrasure.

Above all these emplacements and ramparts rose the three stories of the large Commissioner's House of the 1820s, much to the annoyance of the Royal Engineers. The main entrance into the Keep was across a drawbridge and moat (the residual lagoon of a cave) filled by the sea seeping through the rock. The eastern entrance led into the Caponier of the Southeast Rampart, and from thence into the lower yard of the Keep. Flanking the southern corner of the Keep was the Southeast Rampart, which also covered the drawbridge to the breakwater. This rampart was intended for four guns, two in the face, and two in the flank.

Changes at the Dockyard during the RML era

As part of his 1865 report, which marked the change from smoothbore to rifled artillery, Colonel Jervois reviewed the defenses of the Dockyard. Thus, in the third quarter of the 19th century, the Keep was rearmed with five 10in. RMLs. In the curtains between some of the bastions were an additional seven 64-pdr RMLs. Two new magazines were constructed at the Keep near bastions "C" and "G," with concreted shell-ways to the new RML emplacements. Another 10in. RML was mounted in support of these at Bastion "H," with eight 64-pdr RMLs at Bastion "I" and the Land Front.

The Prospect Hill Position

In his 1865 report, Colonel Jervois discussed the possibility of an enemy landing on the south shore beaches, then proceeding overland to attack the Dockyard from across the Great Sound. In this scenario, the enemy's first object would be to get some guns into position and fire into the Dockyard from Spanish Point, which is at the extremity of a peninsula jutting out westward from the main island of Bermuda and only about 3,000 yards from the Dockyard. To prevent this, it was proposed to construct a line of works to defend against a bombardment from this direction. A favorable position about 7,000 yards distant from the Dockyard was recommended, the principal point of which, Prospect Hill, should be occupied by a defensive line only about a mile long, cutting off the peninsula between the head of Hamilton Harbour and the north shore of the island. The mile-long cordon became known as the "Prospect Hill Position," which comprised, from south to north, forts Hamilton, Prospect, and Langton. Of the three sites, Fort Langton was demolished in the 1980s, Fort Prospect is a water catchment and tank for the City of Hamilton, while Fort Hamilton is a plant nursery with some public access. Each of these three forts is summarized below.

C | **THE DOCKYARD LAND DEFENSES, 1857**

Possibly the last bastioned trace constructed by the Royal Engineers, the defenses for the Royal Naval Dockyard originally covered about 20 acres, with a number of buildings within that area, including the dominating Casemate Barracks (designed to house 320 soldiers), shown here as central to the Land Front, complimented by ordnance stores to either side (the buildings of the dockyard are not shown). The guns of the Land Front looked over three outworks and a glacis that ran from shore to shore at the western end of the Dockyard. The Northwest Rampart protected the dockyard from attack from the sea. The land entrance to the fortifications was by drawbridge to the Couvre Porte, which led to a drawbridge into the South Orillon (anchoring the Land Front on Grassy Bay), while the center was defended by a Ravelin Tower and its Counterguard backed by major ditch. Guarding the right flank of the Land Front was the Right Advance, which has survived, while the other two outworks and South Orillon were lost in 1900–05.

The Royal Naval Dockyard

Fort Hamilton

This fort guarded the southern flank of the Prospect Hill Position and is a pentagonal work erected in the late 1870s. It faces into the head of Hamilton Harbour and across to the Paget shore and easterly to cover the ground between there and the northerly ground toward Fort Prospect. It is a single-period fort and was never rearmed or altered from its original form. There are seven gun emplacements for 64-pdr converted RMLs on Moncrieff disappearing carriages.

Fort Hamilton, overlooking the harbor of the City of Hamilton, was one of the three fortifications of the Prospect Hill Position. With forts Prospect and Langton to the north, it was intended to block an enemy force from reaching Spanish Point, from where the Dockyard could be bombarded almost with impunity. This photo was taken in 1993. (McGovern Collection)

Fort Prospect

This work was the largest of the trio that made up the Prospect Hill Position. Fort Prospect's heptagonal design allowed for 12 64-pdr RMLs on Moncrieff disappearing carriages in double emplacements of three different types.

Fort Langton

The Prospect Hill Position terminated at Fort Langton, completed in 1881, near the north shore of Devonshire Parish. Unlike forts Hamilton and Prospect, which were land forts, Fort Langton was both a land and a coastal battery. To landward and looking down the Devonshire valleys to cross with the coverage from Fort Prospect were four emplacements for 64-pdr RML guns on Moncrieff disappearing carriages. To seaward there were three 10in. RMLs of 18 tons, firing en barbette.

Whale Bay Battery and the Somerset Position

From the central parishes, the Royal Engineers turned their attention westward and to the defense of the rear of the Dockyard: Whale Bay Battery and Scaur Hill Fort.

Whale Bay Battery

In considering the seven minor passages through the Bermuda reef platform during his visit in 1865, Colonel Jervois came to the view that all, excepting Hogfish Cut, were too far from shore to defend with fortifications. The Hogfish Cut runs along the western coast leading to the Dockyard and was of value to local shipping, hence Jervois favored defending that channel with

D KEEP AT THE DOCKYARD, 1878

The Keep was intended to be the area of last refuge, should an enemy (i.e. the United States) take the western Dockyard sector. With seven irregular bastions, it encompasses 10 acres of ground, surmounted by the magnificent Commissioner's House, erected in the 1820s. The Keep was armed and then rearmed in three periods, the first being the last days of the smoothbore cannon, ending in the 1860s. A final phase, starting in the 1890s, saw the installment of BLRs, while depicted here are some of the 10in. RMLs that were emplaced in the 1870s, soon to be made obsolete by BL weapons. The gunners of the RGA are conducting target practice using 15-man gun crews to fire the 400lb shells at a muzzle velocity of 1,364ft/sec for a maximum range of 6,000 yards using 70lb of powder.

Cutting the island of Somerset in two with its ditch, Scaur Hill Fort was erected to cover the passage from the main island of Bermuda at Somerset Bridge of an enemy force intent on attacking the Royal Naval Dockyard using an approach by land, after landing on the beaches of the south coast. This image was taken in 2016. (John Singleton)

batteries mounting RMLs. By 1869, nothing had happened and Jervois made a further recommendation that RMLs be mounted on the site of the old Whale Bay Battery. His plan for Whale Bay was put into action and the battery was completed in the mid-1870s.

Whale Bay Battery was a relatively simple work, not in the polygonal tradition seen at the Prospect Hill Position. Like Alexandra Battery, it is a forerunner of the demise of the fort as a defendable unit. Its three guns, 9in. RMLs of 12 tons, were mounted en barbette in concrete emplacements. Several magazines and stores were located to the rear of the guns; there were apparently no lifts and all ammunition was moved by hand up to the guns. A date-stone over the magazines gives the year 1876.

The Somerset Position: Scaur Hill Fort and ditch

In his 1865 report, which changed the face of Bermuda's fortifications, Colonel Jervois also looked at the approach to the Dockyard from the south. By 1869, the plans were being prepared for the "Somerset Position" at the southeast end of Somerset Island, between the Great Sound and Elys Harbour. As there were only 500 yards between them, they could be most advantageously defended by a continuous ditch and parapet from shore to shore, with a small keep in the center. The result was Scaur Hill Fort and its ditch.

The site had two main components: the fort itself, and the extensive ditch. The ditch was formed by quarrying into the hillside, in several places to a depth of 20ft. From the east, it ran at a right angle from the shoreline of the Great Sound up to the fort itself. It then turned for several angles around the fort and its western gun emplacement, thereafter continuing west in a straight line down to a small beach on Ely's Harbour. Two defensive features protected the ditch, the first being a rampart on its northern side, which was supplied throughout its length with a firing step for infantry. At the fort, two flanking galleries for rifles and cannon fired down several runs of the ditch, while secondary galleries for rifles only added to the protection.

Scaur Hill Fort itself is a hybrid work, which has features of the old polygonal system of fortification combined with the coming era where gun emplacements dominated the plan and any sense of a defensible structure was ultimately lost. The guns, which formed the excuse for building the almost useless fort, also in part suggest the changes of the next generation. The western emplacement is nothing more than a gun behind a parapet and ditch. Both pieces were converted 64-pdr RMLs on Moncrieff disappearing carriages, set in an open-backed emplacement for the western gun and in an enclosed pit for the gun at the fort. No alterations were made to Scaur Hill Fort after the RML period.

Garrison life

Regular soldiers invalided from continental battlefields as part of the Royal Garrison Battalion had been stationed in Bermuda between 1778 and 1784 during the American War of Independence, but were withdrawn following the Treaty of Paris. The Royal Naval establishment began with facilities in the Town of St George's in 1795, and by 1812 Bermuda hosted an Admiralty House and an incipient dockyard, as well as a naval squadron during the winter. Following the French Revolution, a detachment of the 47th Foot was sent to Bermuda in 1793. Regular soldiers would continue to be stationed in Bermuda from then until 1957. With a regular garrison, Bermudians lost interest in maintaining militias. The Militia Acts were allowed to lapse and, other than a brief resurgence during the War of 1812, the Bermuda government would not raise local forces until pressed by the Secretary of State for War to create the Bermuda Militia Artillery (BMA) and the Bermuda Volunteer Rifle Corps (BVRC) eight decades later.

Prospect Camp and Fort Prospect were the center of British Army military activities on Bermuda for almost 100 years. This view from the north was taken in 1955. Today, this property is owned by the government and serve as a school and the Bermuda Police Service headquarters. (NMB Collections)

With the build-up of the Dockyard, there was a corresponding increase in the size of the army garrison that was to protect it. This included the construction of numerous fortifications and coastal artillery batteries, manned by the Royal Artillery (Royal Garrison Artillery, or RGA), and camps where infantry troops were stationed. The Royal Engineers were an important part of the garrison, improving pre-existing fortifications and batteries, building new forts, surveying the island, building a causeway to link St George's Island to the Main Island, a lighthouse at Gibb's Hill, telegraph system, and various other facilities. A system of military roads was built; the rudimentary roads that had existed before had been used by islanders primarily to take the shortest route to the shore, with most passengers and wares moved around the archipelago by boats.

St George's Garrison was a large base including barracks and a hospital, to the east and north of the Town of St George's. Used primarily by the RGA, following the infantry's relocation to Prospect Camp, this large base served the surrounding forts and batteries. Originally, most of the regular soldiers were deployed around St George's, but with the development of the City of Hamilton in the central parishes, which had become the capital in 1815, and of the Dockyard at the West End, it became necessary to redeploy the army westward as well. The heaviest cluster of forts and batteries remained at the East End, where shipping passed in through the reef from the open Atlantic, and this meant that the artillery soldiers continued to concentrate most heavily at the East End. The infantry, however, established a large camp at the center of Bermuda *c.*1855. Located in Devonshire, on the outskirts of Hamilton, it was called **Prospect Camp**. The camp housed other units, as well, including RGA detachments at a fort built within the camp, Fort Prospect. Although Prospect Camp had extensive areas for training, it was surrounded by public roads and residential areas, and had no safe area for a rifle range. Consequently, a second base, **Warwick Camp**, was added primarily to provide rifle ranges to the soldiers of the garrison, and the Dockyard's own Royal Marine detachment (and those of the ships stationed there). Various other smaller sites were used by the army over the history of the garrison. These included Watford Island and the southern half of Boaz Island, both part of the Admiralty land holdings attached to the Dockyard, where **Clarence Barracks** housed a considerable number of soldiers, and Agar's Island, where substantial underground munitions bunkers were built.

Operational history, 1784–1898

The Imperial period in Bermuda was one of continuous improvement of the island as a key British military base in the Western Atlantic. Although the British Empire was engaged in numerous conflicts during this period, none of them directly impacted Bermuda. The fortifications built in Bermuda in the previous five decades reached their maturity (see the Appendix for the forts constructed during this period), particularly regarding their armament, which represented the best and the largest guns at the apogee of the smooth-bore era as shown in Table 1 below.

Table 1: Artillery on Bermuda in the 1850s

Fort/gun	18-pdr	24-pdr	32-pdr	68-pdr (8in.)	Carronade (24-pdr)	Mortar	Howitzer	Totals
Cunningham	-	10	-	-	-	-	-	10
Buildings Bay	-	-	7	-	-	-	-	7
Albert	-	-	7	-	-	2 10in.	2 8in.	11
Catherine	-	5	12	7	2	-	-	26
Victoria	2	18	-	-	-	2 8in.	-	22
Western Redoubt	-	4	-	4	-	-	-	8
George	-	4	-	4	-	-	-	8
Martello	1	-	-	-	-	-	-	1
Dockyard	-	48	27	14	30	4 10in.	-	123
Totals	**3**	**89**	**53**	**29**	**32**	**8**	**2**	**216**

An overall total of 216 pieces in the Defence Report 1857 represents the apex in the number of guns emplaced on Bermuda, while only a few years later Bermuda would face considerable concern over the defenses of the island during the American Civil War and immediately following the Trent affair in November 1861. Thus, in 1857, the number of guns had increased by 81 from the 135 in position at the beginning of the 19th century. Thereafter the numbers would decline as the caliber and power of the new rifled breech, and muzzle-loading guns came into being in the late 1850s and early 1860s. The efficiency of rifled artillery was amply demonstrated during the American Civil War. Coupled with the building of iron-hulled ships, with the French *Gloire* (1859) and the British *Warrior* (1860), shortly to be steam-driven with screw propulsion, the armaments of war changed forever and the unending arms race began. This fundamental sea-change was reflected in a new round of Bermuda fortifications after 1865 (see Appendix). The refortification and rearmament of Bermuda for the RML

FORT CUNNINGHAM, 1880

Built in the 1820s during the smoothbore period and named for its designer, Fort Cunningham was originally constructed of the hard Bermuda limestone and set in a wide ditch with counterscarp galleries. A series of arches of unknown function formed the outer wall of the fort at ditch level. In the 1870s, the entire upper work of the Fort was removed and its smoothbore cannons were replaced with nine RMLs in 12.5, 10 and 9in.

calibers in casemates. The 12.5in. and 10in. calibers were positioned behind straight-fronted, armored Gibraltar Shields and enclosed in wrought-iron casemates (seen in cutaway view). These RML barrels were discovered in 1991 following excavation of the fort's ditch, having been discarded there in 1905. Also discovered at this point was the faded black, red, and yellow painted camouflage from the RML period.

era resulted in the guns listed in Table 2 (excluding smoothbore cannon for ditch defenses).

Table 2: Bermuda artillery in the RML era

Fort	64-pdr	9in. RML	10in. RML	11in. RML	12.5in. RML	Totals
George	2	-	-	2	-	**4**
Victoria	8	-	-	3	-	**11**
Albert	-	-	4	-	-	**4**
Catherine	3	-	5	-	-	**8**
Alexandra	-	5	-	-	-	**5**
Cunningham	-	2	5	-	2	**9**
Hamilton	7	-	-	-	-	**7**
Prospect	6	-	-	-	-	**6**
Langton	4	-	3	-	-	**7**
Whale Bay	-	3	-	-	-	**3**
Scaur Hill	2	-	-	-	-	**2**
Dockyard	15	-	6	-	-	**21**
Totals	**47**	**10**	**23**	**5**	**2**	**87**

By the turn of the century, when the RMLs began to be replaced by the steel breech loaders, the number of guns at Bermuda had been halved. The march of technology, which ushered in the rifled gun of the 1860s and saw the introduction of the projectile, increased not only the range of the weapons, but their size, weight, and caliber. By 1895, 87 pieces did the work of the previous 216. This progression caused by technological advances continued into the new steel breech-loader period of the first decade of the 20th century and as the guns increased in power, their numbers correspondingly continued to decline.

The Western Division was one of the three sectors of the Royal Garrison Artillery (RGA), RA at Bermuda. Of the 104 companies of the RGA, 37 served overseas in the various colonies of the British Empire. Captured in this image are the NCOs of No. 3 Company, Western, which was based at Scaur Hill Fort and manned the 64-pdrs on Moncrieff disappearing carriages in the 1880s. (NMB Collections)

THE 20TH CENTURY, 1899–1995

During the 20th century, Bermuda's defenses would be greatly impacted by technology and global wars (World War 1 and 2, and the Cold War). The military's role on Bermuda would go from its apex in manpower and spending to its nadir when the island's entire military establishment (except for the local Royal Bermuda Regiment) disappeared. Over this century, the United States and France would cease to threaten Britain and Bermuda, replaced by Germany and the Soviet Union.

In the years leading up to World War 1, a worldwide arms race caused Britain to invest heavily in both its navy and army, including the defenses of Bermuda. The actual outbreak of the war drew military resources away from Bermuda, except for those that countered the German U-boat threat. In 1918, Britain emerged as one of the victors, but was financially exhausted, which led to a reduction in its imperial expenditures. The worldwide economic depression of the late 1920s reinforced the decline in Britain's and Bermuda's defenses. Only the coming of World War 2 and the development of new military technologies drove improvements in Bermuda's military infrastructure, but Britain needed to focus its limited resources on its home defenses.

World War 2 led to an impact on Bermuda's defenses as great as when Britain lost the American War of Independence in 1783. In 1941, America assumed the primary role of defending Bermuda. The influx of American manpower and funding would reshape the islands of Bermuda and add many military installations, including coast defenses. Bermuda served as an important link between America and Europe during the war and a key staging point in the battle of the Atlantic against German U-boats and surface raiders.

The war also drained Britain's financial resources, so a reduction in military spending reduced Bermuda's defenses even further, until the Army and Navy had withdrawn most of their forces from Bermuda by the late 1950s. The centerpiece of Bermuda's military mission, the Royal Naval Dockyard, was downsized and would later close in 1995. The Americans continued to maintain and even expand their defense role on Bermuda during the Cold War, as the island became an outpost defending America against Soviet forces, especially submarines. The US no longer needed to maintain its bases on Bermuda with the end of the Cold War, so in 1995 the US and remaining British establishment withdrew their naval and air assets. This brought to an end the military defense of Bermuda after almost 400 years.

Design and development

The Bermuda Defence Report of 1904 stated that, "Bermuda as an Imperial fortress and naval base is being fortified on a scale which is considered sufficient to deter a considerable squadron, including one or two battleships, from engaging the coast defenses." The Americans were still considered a force to be reckoned with and the report went on to say: "All attacks on Bermuda would have as their definite objectives the destruction or capture of the Dockyard at Ireland Island, with coal-yard, stores, floating dock and workshops, or the severing of cable communications." Naval and artillery technology had advanced so much in the short period since Bermuda had been rearmed with RMLs in the last quarter of the 19th century that those defenses had become obsolete. Rifled breech-loading coast artillery with much longer ranges were now needed to counter modern warships, such as the Dreadnought-type of battleship or speedy torpedo boats. The Royal Engineers and Royal Artillery returned to their task of fortifying Bermuda, starting as the century began and ending around 1910 with the construction of a new defensive work at St David's Head. Four sites at the east end and two at the west were eventually drawn into this last major British cycle of the fortification of the Bermuda, which emphasized coast artillery over the fortified structures.

By early 1939, the once numerous coast defenses had been reduced to only two 6in. BL guns at St David's Battery. The early events of World War 2 and the dire situation in which Britain found itself led to the inability of the Crown, overextended in the defense of the empire, to assure the protection of Bermuda, and the mantle passed to the American armed forces. Therefore, the American defensive works at Bermuda represent the last major phase in the history of its coastal defenses. Because of the strength of the British and American forces in the Western North Atlantic, the "local defensive forces in Bermuda need be only strong enough to protect against hostile raids by sea and air." In these statements of late 1941 lay the three main aspects of American works at Bermuda, namely a naval operating base (including seaplanes), an airfield for land-based aircraft, and defense works for the protection of both. The transfer of responsibility for the defense of Bermuda began with an agreement for a seaplane base on Morgan's Island in the Great Sound that was signed on September 1, 1939, two days before Britain declared war on Germany. This agreement evolved into a larger American footprint on Bermuda when on September 2, 1940, the United Kingdom informed the US that it would "secure the grant to the Government of the United States, freely and without consideration, of the [99-year] lease for immediate establishment and use of Naval and Air bases … on the East coast and on the Great Bay [Sound] of Bermuda." An American committee under Admiral John W. Greenslade immediately departed for Bermuda to choose the sites. Matters continued to move rapidly as on November 3, 1940, an American team under Major D.G. White arrived to survey, make land valuations on properties to be purchased, and amass engineering and construction data. The final plans were that Morgan's and Tucker's islands and a part of the main island in Southampton were to become the US Naval Air Station and US Naval Operating Base; Long Bird Island ultimately became US Army Kindley Field, and St David's and Cooper's Island the US Army Fort Bell. Additional parcels of land needed for base end stations and other facilities completed these defenses. American manpower on Bermuda would reach over 6,000 at their peak.

These American defence facilities continued to be used into the Cold War with the Soviet Union, as the Bermuda bases supported the operation of air and naval forces for the protection of air and sea approaches to the United States in the Western Atlantic, and prevented the establishment of an enemy force in these islands.

Tour of the sites and features
The final major round of updating the British fortification of Bermuda took place from 1894 to 1904, when forts Cunningham and Victoria, and Alexandra and St David's batteries (all covering the Narrows Channel to St

The 20th Century, 1899–1995

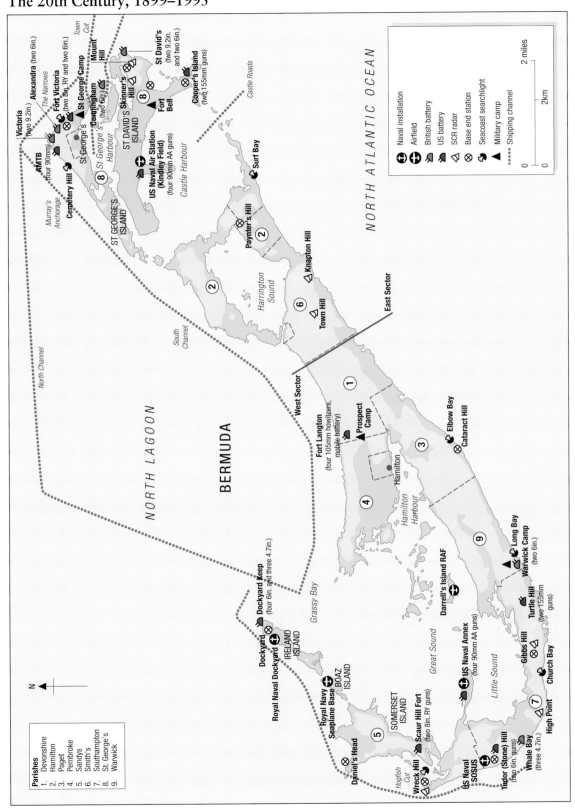

Parishes
1. Devonshire
2. Hamilton
3. Paget
4. Pembroke
5. Sandys
6. Smith's
7. Southampton
8. St. George's
9. Warwick

Alexandra (two 6in.)

Victoria (two 9.2in.)

Fort Victoria (two 8in. RY and two 6in.)

The Narrows

St George Camp

Cuningham (two 6in.)

Mount Hill

St David's (two 9.2in. and two 6in.)

St DAVID'S SKINNER'S HILL

Cooper's Island (two 155mm guns)

Fort Bell

Town Cut

Castle Roads

AMTB (four 90mm)

Cemetery Hill

St George's

St George's Harbour

Murray's Anchorage

ST GEORGE'S ISLAND

US Naval Air Station (Kindley Field) (four 90mm AA guns)

Castle Harbour

Surf Bay

NORTH ATLANTIC OCEAN

Paynter's Hill

Knapton Hill

Harrington Sound

Town Hill

East Sector

South Channel

West Sector

North Channel

NORTH LAGOON

BERMUDA

Fort Langton (four 105mm howitzers, mobile battery)

Prospect Camp

Elbow Bay

Cataract Hill

Hamilton

Hamilton Harbour

Darrell's Island RAF

Long Bay

Warwick Camp (two 6in.)

Turtle Hill (two 155mm guns)

Great Sound

US Naval Annex (four 90mm AA guns)

Little Sound

Gibbs Hill

Church Bay

High Point

Grassy Bay

Dockyard Keep (four 6in. and three 4.7in.)

Dockyard

Royal Naval Dockyard

IRELAND ISLAND

BOAZ ISLAND

Royal Navy Seaplane Base

SOMERSET ISLAND

Scaur Hill Fort (two 8in. RY guns)

Daniel's Head

Wreck Hill

Hogfish Cut

US Naval SOSUS

Whale Bay (three 4.7in.)

Tudor (Stone) Hill (two 6in. guns)

N

Legend:
- Naval installation
- Airfield
- British battery
- US battery
- SCR radar
- Base end station
- Seacoast searchlight
- Military camp
- Shipping channel

0 — 2 miles
0 — 2km

43

George and the Dockyard), as well as Whale Bay Battery and the defenses of the Dockyard each received new coast artillery.

Fort Victoria

On the northern side of Fort Victoria, the Ravelin Tower was buried under a 9.2in. rifled breech loader, one of a pair, the second being about 75ft to the east. Their fire would have crossed with that of Alexandra Battery to the southeast. The new guns remained in use for several years, but by 1910, one had been removed and may have been taken to St David's Battery. By 1935, the remaining gun was not considered part of the Bermuda active defense. The 9.2in. gun at Fort Victoria would remain through its transformation into a resort, to be removed in 2011 to the National Museum of Bermuda.

The 6in. battery at Great Head, St David's Island, in 1986. By the first year of World War 2, these were the only active coast artillery pieces on the island. It mounted two 6in. RBLs with antiaircraft shields (these World War 2 shields were much decayed and removed in recent times). (McGovern Collection)

St David's Battery (shown here in 2007) is now under the auspices of Bermuda's National Parks. On the left are the two rifles of 9.2in. caliber, while the pair of 6in. RBLs lie a little to the east. All of these were intended to protect the entrance to the Narrows Channel, and the 6in. guns remained operational until the end of British coastal defense in 1957. (NMB Collections)

Alexandra Battery

To the southeast of Fort Victoria, the works of the 1870s at Alexandra Battery were swept away and replaced by two 6in. BL rifles in concrete emplacements with a glacis extending down to the shoreline. Constructed by 1899, the guns appear to have been out of use before World War 1, as they do not appear in the Defence Report for 1913. The site was not used in World War 2.

Fort Cunningham

The initial replacement plan proposed to leave the two 12.5in. RMLs at Fort Cunningham and to add two 6in. BL rifles. By that date, one of the 9in. RMLs had already been removed and the second must have been taken away shortly thereafter. It was subsequently decided to remove all of the RMLs and they were dropped into the northern ditch from the roof of the fort. The ditch had already been partly filled up in the late 1880s, but that work was entirely covered by the soils of the glacis for the BL guns, which had been placed on the roof of the fort. The glacis was contoured to allow five of the RML gun ports to be used as windows, for the old RML casemates were turned into barracks. The weapons do not appear as operational in the 1913 Defense Report and were not included at all in a 1935 battery return.

St David's Battery

The only entirely new work to be erected in the rearmament of Bermuda in the first decade of the 20th century was the battery of four guns on St David's Island in 1907. The weapons were to be two 6in. and two 9.2in. BL guns, which were made available by moving existing coast artillery from other Bermuda locations. One of these 6in. guns was taken from the Keep at Ireland Island, and another of the same caliber from Alexandra Battery. It appears that one of the 9.2in. guns came from storage at the ordnance yard at Ireland Island. The other 9.2in. gun was most likely relocated from the eastern side of the 9.2in. battery at Fort Victoria. Supporting these guns were searchlight stations and position-finding cells. By 1935, the two 9.2in. guns at St David's Battery were no longer mentioned in defense reports. The two 6in. BLs became the only British guns at the East End during World War 2.

Along with the Keep at the Dockyard, Whale Bay Battery was the only fortification on the western side of Bermuda that was upgraded in 1900 to the new breech-loading artillery. In this case, the battery was home to three 4.7in. QF guns, intended to cover Hogfish Cut Channel that led to the western reaches of the Royal Naval Dockyard. This image was taken in 2016. (John Singleton)

Whale Bay Battery and the Dockyard

The western defenses were also modified at Whale Bay Battery and the Dockyard. The three 9in. RML emplacements at Whale Bay were built over to take three 4.7in. Quick-Firing (QF) BL pieces. The original purpose of the battery to protect the entrance to Hogfish Cut Channel was unchanged, as it was through that rear entrance to the Dockyard that torpedo boats could have attacked. By 1913 and the beginning of World War 1, Whale Bay Battery ceased to be an operational unit and was not used in the 1939–45 conflict.

At the Dockyard, most of the modifications took place at the Keep, which by 1906 mounted seven new guns, only two 12-pdr QF guns being erected on the land front. At bastions "A" and "B," facing southeast, and "G," facing west, three 4.7in. QF guns were emplaced against torpedo boats and light craft. Between these, bastions "C" through "F" mounted four 6in. BL rifles facing the channel to Grassy Bay from St Catherine's Point and northward towards the reefs and the open sea. In the 1913 report, one of the 6in. guns had disappeared, and three were operational; all were out of use by 1935.

Coastal batteries on Bermuda between the World Wars

The demands of the British Empire for military resources and the rapid advance of naval technology during World War 1 resulted in coastal batteries constructed only a few years before becoming obsolete or placed in caretaker status due to the lack of manpower. In 1928, the regular Royal Artillery units and the Royal Engineers Fortress Company were withdrawn, with their roles taken up respectively by the Bermuda Militia Artillery (BMA) and the new Bermuda Volunteer Engineers (BVE), raised in 1931. The coastal artillery forts and batteries were all mothballed or permanently removed except for **St David's Battery**, which continued in the role of Examination Battery, watching over the shipping channel through Bermuda's surrounding barrier reef. The regular army infantry battalion was replaced by a company detached from whichever battalion was deployed to Jamaica. This consequently increased the requirement for part-time infantrymen. As the manpower requirements of the artillery had been reduced with the closure of most of the batteries, a new unit, the Bermuda Militia Infantry (BMI), was raised, grouped administratively with the BMA and likewise recruiting black soldiers, in 1939.

Sensing the approach of a new war, and realizing that the Dockyard, some miles to the north of Warwick Camp, was vulnerable to naval bombardment, it was decided to build a battery at the highest point within

The Keep at the Royal Naval Dockyard was substantially rearmed for the breech-loading period of artillery at the end of the 1800s, though its guns were dismantled in the early 1920s. It mounted three 4.7in. QF guns and four 6in. RBLs, and covered the channel to the Dockyard and the City of Hamilton beyond. This photo was taken in 1943. (NMB Collections)

Warwick Camp, with two 6in. BL guns formerly installed at Fort Cunningham. Both guns were refurbished, but only one was operational when local forces were mobilized on September 3, 1939, for the start of World War 2. Although the guns of most naval ships outranged the elderly 6in. guns, it was thought that the Warwick Camp was far enough to the south of the Dockyard to prevent ships coming near enough to shell it. From that location, the guns could also repel any raiding parties that attempted to cross the reef line in small boats to land on the beaches below. As with St David's Battery, the guns were manned by the BMA and the defense electric lights by the BVE. Until mid-1941, those two batteries represented the full strength of the coastal defenses of Bermuda.

US seacoast defense works

When the first American force arrived in Bermuda, they reported back to Washington that Bermuda was defended from the sea by only four 6in. guns. The ground defenses against landing parties at such vital places as the oil dock, the cable head, and the radio station were at the bare minimum. There were no antiaircraft guns on the island, nor even machine guns except a few .30-cal. machine guns carried by the infantry. The Americans' early priority was to provide coast artillery and manpower to shore up these defenses.

The first US land forces to Bermuda were under the command of Colonel Alden G. Strong (US Army commander of the Bermuda Base Command), who arrived on the USS *American Legion* in Hamilton on April 20, 1941, along with 860 men of Company G, 11th Infantry; Battery F, 52nd Coast Artillery; and Battery B, 57th Coast Artillery, with four 8in. railway guns and four 155mm GPF (*Grande Puissance Filloux*) guns. Within hours of disembarking, Colonel Strong had drawn up a joint plan with Captain Jules James (commander of the US Naval Operating Base) for the defense of Bermuda. The railway guns were to be placed at the two ends of the chain of islands, one battery on Somerset Island, the other at St George's. The 155mm guns covered the ground between, with a battery at Cooper's Island and another in Southampton Parish. The value of the American weapons was in their range. The British 6in. guns had a maximum range of 11,000 yards, compared with that of the 155mm at 17,400 yards and the 8in. railway gun at 23,900 yards.

F   **ST. DAVID'S BATTERY, 1915**

Bermuda is surrounded by a curtain of reefs, and there has only been one channel for large ships through these natural defenses, aptly called the Narrows (at the eastern end of Bermuda). The Narrows became the major focus of the defense of the island, after the Dockyard itself. The advance of military technology made the forts and batteries of St George's and Paget islands obsolete, so St David's Battery was erected to replace them on the Great Head on St David's Island. Completed before the start of World War 1, the battery contained a pair of 6in. and a pair of 9.2in. BL guns (all four survive in place, making this coastal battery one of the few in the world to have retained its guns for their entire service life). This view shows the gunners of the RGA and BMA holding their annual live fire drill on the 9.2in. guns. These Mark X guns could fire a 380lb shell on the Mark V mounting at a maximum elevation of 15 degrees to a maximum range of 21,000 yards.

Scaur Hill Fort was the site for the western 8in. railway battery. To the northwest of its entrance stood a sloping water catch above which was placed one 8in. railway gun. The second gun of this battery was probably on an adjacent hillock to the northeast. Fort Victoria was on St George's Island and to its east lay Fort Albert. On the slope between the two, facing the Narrows Channel, the two US railway guns were cut into the hillside. Emplacing these 8in. Model 1888 M.II guns on Model 1918 MI carriages without a railway required the guns to be permanently located by installing a short section of track at each site. The 8in. railway guns were complemented by a two-gun 155mm GPF battery at Turtle Hill and another at Cooper's Island. The 155mm GPF Model 1918 guns had been placed on concrete Panama Mounts by the end of October 1941, allowing these field guns to track moving warships.

In April 1942, a second phase of American defenses commenced with the construction of concrete emplacements for two 6in. M1903A2 guns on Model BC M1 carriages with armored shields, and an intervening support bunker at Tudor Hill on the west coast, a few miles south of Scaur Hill Fort. **Battery Construction No. 284** was completed in May 1943; the guns were installed by mid-August. At Tudor Hill, the eastern emplacement and plotting, power, and magazine bunker remain today. The western emplacement appears to have been destroyed or buried in the development of the site by the US Navy for sonar testing facilities. Covering the eastern end of Bermuda and its seaward approaches, **Battery Construction No. 283** was a similar two-gun emplacement at Fort Victoria. In the 1960s, the property which includes forts Victoria and Albert was leased to a hotel chain, and new works in 1984 led to the destruction of both the northern and southern emplacement, while the plotting, power, and magazine bunker still exists (with its rear entrance built into the side of Fort Victoria's ditch). Overlooking Murray Anchorage from the left flank of Fort Victoria, the Americans installed an **Anti-Motor Torpedo Boat Battery** (AMTB) mounting four 90mm guns.

By 1942, the American and British seacoast defense was organized and manned by the 27th Coast Artillery Battalion (Harbor Defense) (Comp), augmented by the men of the two British batteries, under the commanding officer of the 27th Coast Artillery Battalion, headquartered at Burrow's Hill at Fort Bell, and was divided into East and West groups. In late 1943, the four 6in. guns, one battery in each group, came into operation, giving a grand total of 16 pieces of coast artillery under the Bermuda Base Command After the modern 6in. batteries (which had a range of fire to 27,000 yards) were installed and manned, the railway guns were withdrawn. (See the Appendix for a listing of batteries.)

The fire control system for the batteries consisted of a series of 13 base end stations. Ten sites have been identified, two of which, Gibbs and Mount hills, apparently had two stations each. Working from east to west, the base end stations were: Fort Victoria, Mount Hill, Cooper's Island, Paynter's Hill, Cataract Hill, Gibbs Hill, Tudor Hill, Wreck Hill, Daniel's Head, and HM Dockyard. Daniel's Head, Gibbs Hill, Paynter's Hill, and Mount Hill are still standing. High Point and Skinners Hill stations had radar type SCR-296 (range 50,000 yards), while Gibbs and Mount hills had SCR-582. Ten searchlight emplacements for the coast artillery were located on Bermuda.

Antiaircraft artillery

The American bases were defended by antiaircraft weapons. Kindley Field was defended by four 90mm guns and four .50-cal. machine guns manned by Battery B, 423rd Coast Artillery Battalion (AA), at Burrow's Hill. Other groups of the 423rd were at Whalebone Bay at the western end of St George's Island, and at the Oil Docks, next to Cemetery Hill. They also controlled other guns at the airfield and Mount Hill. In the western end, the Naval Operating Base was defended by four 90mm guns at the Glebe in Southampton, with four .50-cal. machine guns for local defense (Battery C, 423rd Coast Artillery Battalion). Battery E comprised a dozen .50-cal. AA machine guns, at the Dockyard, and around King's Point (Naval Operating Base—NOB).

At least ten AAA searchlight sections from Battery A, 423rd Coast Artillery Battalion (Comp) (AA), were sited around the island. Antiaircraft SCR-268 radars were located at Whalebone Bay, and Turtle and Tudor hills. Each was specifically sited to provide early-warning information to an operations center, known as the "Central Training School," which was located near the Middle Road at Prospect Barracks. Longer-range radar coverage for Bermuda was tackled by a series of stations for the Air Warning Service, under the 693rd Signal Aircraft Warning Company, with detectors SCR-516-C at Mount and Knapton hills, with long-range detectors of the type SCR-271 installed at Town Hill and at Cove Point, St David's.

At the Southlands estate on the south coast of Warwick Parish, US forces established an antiaircraft training school. This photo taken from a British plane captures the unit in action during 1943, with four different types of AA guns blazing and smoke filling the air. Most of the targets were towed behind RAF planes (NARA)

Land and other defense measures

A Land Defense Task Group was organized in several sectors of the island. This group consisted of US Marines, the Canadian Pictou Highlanders, the Bermuda Militia Infantry, and the Bermuda Volunteer Rifle Corps. The Harrington Sound Sector was thought vital to the defense of Kindley Field, and was assigned to the general reserve, the second part of the land forces, consisting of the 3rd Battalion, 89th Infantry, and Battery A, 214th Field Artillery Battalion. The infantry would be assembled near Harrington Sound in an emergency, supported by

The Bermuda Militia Artillery, associated with the Royal Garrison Artillery, was a local volunteer force that manned the guns at St David's Battery in the two World Wars. Here the men are training prior to World War 2, when the site became the Examination Battery for ships seeking to enter the Narrows Channel to the Dockyard, the Great Sound, and the City of Hamilton. (NMB Collections)

During World War 2, the RAF established a seaplane base at Darrell's Island on the southern reaches of the Great Sound of Bermuda. Originally built for commercial transatlantic clippers, it was also used by the US Navy while the Naval Operation Base was being constructed. The base was used throughout the war and was instrumental in ferrying many personnel across the Atlantic. The photo was taken in 1945. (NARA)

Battery A, 214th Field Artillery Battalion, from Fort Langton, with four 105mm howitzers on towed carriages. This battery occupied Fort Langton from June 1942 until April 1943.

In addition to the artillery and air defense of Bermuda, there were several other military facilities of note. The naval air station at Southampton was home to a fleet of flying boats that patrolled the sealanes. There was a submarine base established at Ordnance Island in St George's Harbour, from which patrols covered the Bermuda area. Several torpedo boats operated out of the NOB in the Great Sound. Once Kindley Field had been constructed, there were land-based patrol bombers. At Fort St Catherine, there was a magnetic loop control station for the detection of submarines. At "Southlands" on the south coast of Warwick Parish, a major antiaircraft training center (AATC) was established for the practice firing of 40mm twin Bofors, and 20mm and 3in. AA guns, as well as machine guns.

Garrison life

The manpower needs of the Boer wars and then World War 1 drained Bermuda of regular army units, leading to a reduction of the active defenses and use of local militia to man the remaining defenses. Troops from Canada were called upon to fill the gap and a succession of Canadian battalions would serve for a time on Bermuda. They were replaced by a British Territorial Force unit, the 2/4th Battalion of the East Yorkshire Regiment, for the remainder of the conflict.

During World War 2, as had been the case during World War 1, the British units posted to Bermuda to provide the regular infantry company on garrison included reserve units from the Canadian Army embodied for the war. The part-time units were once again mobilized for the duration. Conscription was quickly introduced, with all military-age British male residents in Bermuda liable for service. In addition to maintaining guards at the Dockyard and Darrell's Island, the infantry soldiers guarded the transatlantic cable facilities, beaches, and inlets, patrolled the island, and operated motor boat patrols.

G   US BATTERY No. 284, 1943

Constructed by the US Army in 1943 as part of the permanent American coastal defenses of Bermuda (to protect the naval operation base/air station and army airfield), Battery Construction No. 284 (the cutaway shows the supporting underground magazines, plotting room, telephone room, and power rooms) mounted two 6in. shielded barrette guns (M1903A2 guns on Model BC M1 carriages) which could fire in any direction, up to 27,000 yards. These guns replaced the temporary two 8in. railway guns (Model 1888 MII guns on Model 1981 MI railway carriages) each on short sections of rail track located between forts Victoria and Albert, with supporting earthen magazines and plotting rooms. The underground portion of Battery No. 284 remains today with access from the ditch of Fort Victoria, but its two emplacements and all the remains of the 8in. railway battery have been removed as part of a hotel development in the 1970s.

Photographed from the air probably in the early 1950s, the Naval Operating Base in Southampton (later known at the US Naval Air Station Annex) was established in 1941 by joining two islands with the mainland at King's Point. It remained operational for over 50 years until the American forces withdrew from Bermuda in the mid-1990s. (NMB Collections)

Captured by the US Navy off the west coast of Africa, the German submarine *U-505* is seen here entering Bermuda waters in June 1944. It was kept secluded at the Naval Operating Base for the rest of World War 2, but is now a memorial to US servicemen at the Museum of Science and Technology in Chicago, Illinois. (NARA)

In addition to the British Army and Royal Navy units in Bermuda during the war, a Royal Canadian Navy base, HMCS Somers Isles, operated at the former Royal Naval site at Convict Bay, and four airbases operated in Bermuda: the Royal Navy's Fleet Air Arm had a seaplane base on Boaz Island; the Royal Air Force used the seaplane base Darrell's Island; the US Navy operated flying boats from the US Naval Operating Base; and the US Army Air Force and the RAF shared Kindley Field. Although air and naval units based in Bermuda played an active part in the battle of the Atlantic, the Axis powers never dared to launch a direct attack on the colony.

Following the end of World War 2, the BVE and BMI ceased to exist. The BMA and BVRC were both demobilized, and reduced to skeleton staffs. Both were quickly built back up to strength in 1951, and conscription, which had been used during the war, was reintroduced for both units (the BVRC being retitled the Bermuda Rifles), although the conscripts served on a part-time basis. The last coastal artillery, the examination battery on St David's Head, was removed from use in 1953, and the BMA converted to infantry, but remained nominally part of the Royal Regiment of Artillery. In 1951, it was announced that the Dockyard would be reduced, with much of its establishment withdrawn immediately. In November 1952, it was decided to withdraw the regular army garrison, too, which was completed by May 1, 1953.

Bermuda maintained both territorial units until 1965, at which time they were amalgamated into the Royal Bermuda Regiment. Although trained in conventional light infantry tactics, the regiment has sought new roles to justify the expenditure required to maintain it, including readiness for internal security roles supporting the Bermuda Police Service, providing hurricane relief in Bermuda and other British territories, and playing an increasing role in maritime patrol. It has also taken on responsibility for providing ceremonial parades that previously had chiefly fallen on the professional soldiers.

Operational history, 1899–1995

Late Victorian era and World War 1

In the opening decade of the 20th century, RGA units were retrained but reduced in size to man the four coast artillery batteries on the East End as well as Whale Bay Battery and the batteries in the Dockyard Keep, while during the Anglo-Boer War (1899–1902),

Bermuda received and housed a total of 5,000 Boer prisoners of war on five of its islands. It should be noted that beside coast artillery, Bermuda was defended during this period by submarine mines located in the primary shipping channels, such as the Narrows. The Royal Engineers' 27th Company (Submarine Mining) was assigned to Bermuda in 1888 to tend the underwater mine defenses from the Royal Army Service Corps docks in Hamilton and St George's.

The Royal Navy establishment on Bermuda changed during this period as the Navy withdrew from Halifax to Bermuda in 1905 and the Halifax Naval Yard was handed over to the Royal Canadian Navy in 1910. During World War 1, the station and its warships found themselves protecting Allied merchant shipping, primarily from German submarines. The vessels of the North America and West Indies Station tracked down German surface raiders and escorted convoys that were assembled at Bermuda before crossing the Atlantic.

World War 2

During World War 2, the British Admiralty in Bermuda again organized transatlantic convoys. Ships would arrive at Bermuda to await sailings for Europe, and once assembled were joined at sea with convoys originating at Halifax, Nova Scotia. The Royal Navy's Fleet Air Arm on Boaz Island, nominally an aircraft repair and replacement facility without its own aircrews, provided air patrols during the early years of the war, using Supermarine Walrus flying boats. Once the US Navy began flying air patrols in 1941, however, RN air patrols ceased. Although the Royal Naval Dockyard had warships assigned to its naval base, her warships were spread across the Atlantic, unable to provide local defense. To enhance the defense of the island, two new bases were constructed by the Allies: a US Navy base to cater for both shipping and flying boats, and a United States Army Air Forces airfield to allow landplanes to use Bermuda as a transatlantic staging post in addition to seaplanes.

The US Naval Operating Base became a peninsula created by leveling and joining Morgan's and Tucker's islands and connecting them to the mainland at King's Point, creating a base with about 260 acres. The naval air station served seaplanes such as PBY Catalinas and PBM Mariners. The base continued to be used for this purpose until 1965, when the last flying boats were withdrawn from service. The US Army established Fort Bell on St David's Island. This

Kindley Field, named for World War 1 airplane ace Captain Field E. Kindley, was constructed between 1941 and 1942. The site also housed the US Army base known as Fort Bell; it was later taken over by the US Navy, and used for antisubmarine air patrols against the Soviets in the Cold War as the US Naval Air Station Bermuda. The base was closed in 1995. (NARA)

As photographed by departing Executive Officer Naval Operating Base Bermuda, Commander Douglas Chamberlin USN, on September 6, 1955, a squadron of six Martin P5M Marlin seaplanes are shown here on deck as part of the task force engaged in tracking Soviet submarines passing by Bermuda during the first decade of the Cold War. (NMB Collections)

During World War 2, seaplanes from the US Naval Operating Base patrolled the seas around Bermuda on the lookout for German submarines. This search function was later taken over by P-3C Orions, operating out of NAS Bermuda (formerly Kindley AFB), instead seeking out Soviet submarines on their way to Cuba or lurking off the East Coast of the United States. The image was taken in 1985. (NARA)

As part of the Cold War activity on Bermuda against Soviet submarines, Argus Island was built in 1960 on a seamount at the western extremity of the plateau of the island. From there cables were laid on the floor of a major trench near Bermuda, into which the Soviet submarines dropped to escape air detection; the cables recorded the noise signature of the Soviet boats and sent that information to the NAVFAC Bermuda and thence to Norfolk, Virginia. (NARA)

base was originally to host the engineers building the airfield, which was achieved by levelling Long Bird Island and other smaller isles and rocks, infilling waterways, and creating a single landmass contiguous with St David's Island on the north side of Castle Harbour. An essential factor on both bases was the dredging of Castle Harbour to provide rock and sand for a landfilling operation, which eventually joined Kindley Field and Fort Bell into a single entity covering 1,165 acres. Construction of buildings began in 1941 and by the end of 1943, when Kindley Field and Fort Bell were largely completed, the cost had reached a little over $40 million. Kindley Field was a facility of the US Army Air Forces, whereas Fort Bell was the province of the US Army ground forces. The American flag was raised on Kindley Field on July 4, 1941, and on November 29, the landing field was declared open for traffic. Antisubmarine patrols of the USAAF staged out of Kindley Field, beginning in April 1942 and ending in February 1944. Thereafter, Kindley Field served transient aircraft between the base at the Azores and the US, handled passengers, cargo, and mail, and furnished air-sea rescue when necessary, which remained a part of its role for the next 25 years.

The Cold War

After World War 2, Bermuda's importance to the Admiralty diminished rapidly. With little remaining interest in policing the world's waterways, and with the American bases to guard Bermuda, the Royal Navy closed most of the Dockyard facilities in 1958 (a process which had begun with the removal of the floating dry dock in 1951), with most of the Admiralty's landholdings in Bermuda (along with all the British Army's properties) being transferred to the local government for £750,000. The South Yard was retained as a supply station, HMS Malabar, and the former Royal Navy wireless facility at Daniel's Head were used by the Royal Canadian Navy. Both of those were closed, along with the US Navy facilities in Bermuda, in 1995. The closure of HMS Malabar marked the end of 200 years of Royal Navy presence on Bermuda.

Following the end of hostilities, US Army forces were withdrawn, other than those required for the defense of Fort Bell and Kindley Field. The airfield ceased to be distinguished within the base, as the name Fort Bell was discontinued and Kindley Field came to be applied to the entire facility. The US Army left Bermuda in 1948, when the US Army Air Force became the independent United States Air Force, and the airfield became Kindley Air Force Base (AFB). The US Air Force continued to operate the base, primarily as a refueling station for transatlantic flights by Military Air Transport Service (MATS) and Strategic Air Command (SAC) aircraft.

One of the earliest acts of renovation and restoration of the British defenses of Bermuda came in the mid-1950s, when the four RMLs at Fort Albert were moved to Fort St Catherine. Members of the Trade Development Board are pictured here with the team of Bermudians who completed the heavy move from Fort Albert. (NMB Collections)

At the same time, the US Navy was still operating antisubmarine air patrols with P5M/SP-5B Marlin seaplanes from Naval Air Station (NAS) Bermuda. Whereas World War 2 air patrols had protected merchant shipping in the Atlantic, the Cold War patrols aimed to guard US cities from Soviet submarines armed with ballistic missiles. The Martin flying boats the Navy had used since the 1950s were withdrawn and replaced by landplanes. During the Cuban Missile Crisis, land-based P-2 Neptune and P-3A Orion reconnaissance flights tracked Soviet shipping in the Atlantic from NAS Bermuda. By the 1960s, with the increase in ranges of aircraft, Kindley's usefulness to the USAF had rapidly diminished. In 1965, the US Navy moved its air operations to Kindley AFB, flying land-based Neptunes and Orions. The airfield was permanently transferred to the US Navy in 1970, operating until 1995 as NAS Bermuda.

During the latter stages of the Cold War, the US Navy would normally station a patrol squadron of nine P-3C Orion aircraft on six-month rotations. These squadrons were frequently augmented by Naval Air Reserve aircraft, as well as NATO/Allied support consisting of Royal Air Force Hawker Siddeley Nimrod MR2s, Canadian Armed Forces CP-140 Auroras, and similar maritime patrol and reconnaissance aircraft from other NATO nations. Following the US Navy's takeover of Kindley AFB, the previous NAS Bermuda was renamed the NAS Annex and served primarily as a dock area for visiting US naval vessels and as a support facility for the nearby Naval Facility (NAVFAC) Bermuda that supported the Sound Surveillance System (SOSUS) activity. The US Navy operated a listening post from Tudor's Hill, in Southampton Parish, from 1954 until the closure of US bases in 1995. This base remotely monitored SOSUS sensors listening for submarines. Also associated with this effort was the manmade Argus Island (a steel tower located 20 miles offshore).

Following the dissolution of the Soviet Union in 1991, the US naval air detachment at Bermuda had been reduced from a full squadron to an average of three P-3B or P-3C aircraft, plus UH-1N Twin Huey search and rescue helicopters. Subsequently, all three US naval bases in Bermuda were closed in 1995. The Bermudian government took over Kindley AFB in 1995 as the Bermuda International Airport, the Island's air link to the rest of the world.

Summary

The rearmament of the Bermuda forts in the first decade of the 20th century affected five earlier works and saw the construction of a single new one (see the Appendix). Around 1913, with all the works emplaced, only 19 guns now protected this imperial fortress.

Table 3: Summary of guns on Bermuda, c.1913

Fort	12-pdr QF	4.7in. QF	6in. BL	9.2in. BL	Totals
Victoria	-	-	-	1	1
Alexandra	-	-	1	-	1
Cunningham	-	-	2	-	2
St David's	-	-	2	2	4
Whale Bay	-	3	-	-	3
Dockyard	2	3	3	-	8
Totals	**2**	**6**	**8**	**3**	**19**

In September 1939, only the two 6in. BL guns at St David's Battery were in operation. The final British work was constructed at Warwick Camp, for two 6in. BL guns, manufactured 40 years before for Fort Cunningham, but re-tubed for the new hostilities. During World War 2, the Americans brought in 12 coastal artillery pieces to Bermuda. The caliber and placement of these British and American weapons are given in Table 4.

Table 4: British and American guns on Bermuda, c.1945

Fort	6in. British	155mm GPF	6in. USA	8in. railway	Totals
Victoria	-	-	2	2	4
St David's	2				2
Cooper's Island	-	2	-	-	2
Warwick Camp	2	-	-	-	2
Turtle Hill	-	2	-	-	2
Tudor Hill	-	-	2	-	2
Scaur Hill	-	-	-	2	2
Totals	**4**	**4**	**4**	**4**	**16**

The American railway guns were removed by 1944 and the remainder of their weapons were taken away shortly after the war. With the closure of the RN base, HMS Malabar, on March 31, 1995, Bermuda's direct connection with a British military presence in the islands ceased (as did the American military presence, in the same year), ending an association that began with the posting of a small garrison in 1701 and that had endured almost 300 years.

AFTERMATH, 1995–PRESENT

Following the disestablishment of the military on Bermuda, there has been a slow decline in the forts, batteries, and bases there. Many of the fortifications became technically obsolete long before 1995. In the early 1950s, the Bermuda government acquired most of the vacant British properties. With the exception of forts St Catherine, Gates, and Scaur Hill, most of the fixed defense works were left to the depredations of the climate, vandals, and official neglect.

Moving from east to west, Fort Victoria was devastated by the building of a resort on its northeast flank in the late 1960s, thus unnecessarily destroying significant parts of the most important fort on St George's Island for a swimming pool and nightclub. Fort Cunningham was converted for a period after World War 2 into a detention center for wayward boys, but fell into decline thereafter. Fort William became a restaurant for several decades after 1960, but that venture has failed and the site remains unattended and much attacked by vegetation, a fate all too familiar throughout Bermuda. Fort George was partly reused as the base for Bermuda Harbour Radio, which monitors shipping in and around the island, but little funding has been put into the preservation of the barracks block upon which it has been superimposed. St David's Battery received some attention in the first decade of this millennium, but the salt-laden climate has taken a considerable toll on its four guns. Alexandra Battery remains static, while Fort Albert received some attention in the 1990s, but is now subject to a slow decline. The St George Camp has been absorbed into the Town of St George's through reuse or removal. Forts St Catherine and Gates and the Martello Tower remain the best cared for at the eastern end of Bermuda.

In the central parishes, Fort Langton was demolished in 1984 and Fort Prospect was turned into a water catchment and tankage for the City of Hamilton. The adjacent Prospect Camp had some of its grand barracks demolished to make way for a school, and Admiralty House, a few miles to the west, was destroyed in the early 1970s. Fort Hamilton was eventually taken over by the Corporation of Hamilton and the three 18-ton RMLs from Fort Langton were moved there in the 1960s. Moving to the western part of Bermuda, Whale Bay Battery and Scaur Hill Fort are in reasonable condition, with the latter receiving considerable attention in recent years as part of Bermuda's national park system.

The 20 acres of massive defenses of the Royal Naval Dockyard at Ireland Island suffered damage when two of its outwork forts were demolished in building a South Yard to accommodate larger warships around 1905. The North Yard was abandoned in 1951, but the fortifications remained largely intact and their surviving 16 acres now form the National Museum of Bermuda. Much work has been done, and continues to be done, by that heritage institution to preserve, enhance, and exhibit those defense works. Of the World War 2 defenses, most of the NOB, except for Battery 283 at Tudor Hill, has been destroyed. At the NAR (Kindley Field and Fort Bell), a number of buildings have been demolished.

VISITING THE SITES TODAY

Under the direction of Andrew Pettit of the National Parks, the two 6in. RBL guns that were emplaced in 1939 at the battery at Warwick Camp were moved to Alexandra Battery. The plan was to mount them in the 6in. emplacements at that battery, as they were not accessible to the public at Warwick Camp. They are waiting for a large crane to lift them into their original emplacements. (Martin Buckley Collection)

The ongoing preservation of the fortifications of the four centuries of military activity at Bermuda is tied to the tourism industry. Of the several hundred guns that were once on Bermuda, over 150 pieces have survived and many are on view. Of the 90-odd fortifications and military venues, several dozen have made it into modern times, in varying degrees of preservation. When visiting Bermuda, the following sites can be seen, although some require access permission, while others need waterborne transportation. The Appendix provides further details on the current status of Bermuda's forts and batteries.

The eastern sector
The following can be visited by land, primarily on the islands of St George's and St David's. Following the coast road out of the Town of St George's, one

can stop at Gate's Fort, Alexandra Battery, and Fort St Catherine. The latter is open to the public and contains displays of historic artillery and other exhibitions, as well as the structure itself, from gun emplacements to underground power and shell magazines. Access to forts Victoria, Albert, and Western Redoubt, as well as the American defenses of Retreat Hill, may be restricted as they are on private property. On the way to Ferry Reach and the Martello Tower, the terreplein at Fort George can be viewed, but the barracks is restricted as it is the home of Bermuda Harbour Radio. On St David's Island, the wonderful coast artillery at St David's Battery is open to the public, while one can drive through parts of former NAS Bermuda (Kindley Field), where some buildings have survived.

In the 1991 excavations of the ditch at Fort Cunningham, conducted by Drs Richard Gould and Edward Harris, with an Earthwatch team, seven RMLs were discovered. The group comprises five 10in. guns weighing 18 tons and two 12.5in. of 25 tons. When obsolete in the 1890s, the barrels were dropped into the ditch and covered over. (NMB Collections)

Three of Bermuda's earliest forts are on Castle Island to the south of Bermuda airport, in one of the prettiest areas of water in all of Bermuda can be accessed by boat. Southampton Fort may be viewed on an adjacent island, but is out of bounds to the public, as the island is a restricted nature reserve. Entering St George's Harbour from the sea by its original channel next to St David's Island, the remains of Smith's Fort may be seen on the left, while those of Paget Fort are on the right. Mooring at the quay on the western side of Paget Island just off the channel, a short walk leads to Fort Cunningham with its magnificent iron frontage.

The central sector
The center of the main island of Bermuda has Fort Hamilton, which is usually open to the public, while Fort Prospect (and Prospect Camp) is somewhat restricted as it lies within a Bermuda Police service camp. Warwick Camp may be seen from the road on the way to the Western Sector.

The western sector
Whale Bay Battery is accessed through the National Park, rather than the adjacent golf course. Moving westward and then northeast, over Somerset Bridge, Scaur Hill Fort is on the highest part of Somerset Island with magnificent views into the Great Sound to the south and northwards over the reefs, which extend out some 8 miles from that part of Bermuda. A wonderful replica Moncrieff disappearing carriage is displayed in an original emplacement.

Bermuda's largest fortifications are on Ireland Island, north from Scaur Hill, and encircle the marvelous buildings of the former Royal Naval Dockyard. The surviving fortifications comprise some 16 acres and all are within the National Museum of Bermuda, though some areas are restricted, due to restoration work. The Keep, at 9.5 acres, is the biggest fort in Bermuda and houses a major military exhibition, as well as the largest collection of historic artillery on Bermuda. Displays on the Royal Bermuda Regiment in the great Commissioner's House bring one into modern times.

Lance Furbert, the former Curator of Bermuda's Forts, stands in front of the rear entrances to US Battery No. 284 in Fort Victoria's ditch, in 1986. (McGovern Collection)

RECOMMENDED READING

Little attention was paid in literary works to the fortifications of Bermuda until the early 1950s, although there were a series of official reports on the defenses up to World War 2. The latter can be accessed through the National Archives at Kew in London, but they may be eventually published by the National Museum of Bermuda. Records on the American defenses of Bermuda are available through the US National Archives and Records Administration in College Park, Maryland.

In the late 1920s, Colonel Roger Willock, as a young man, visited Bermuda and studied its defenses, which resulted in his 1950s', privately published *Bulwark of Empire*, later reprinted by the Bermuda Maritime Museum Press, but now out of print. Willock's book deals largely with the garrisons, with some emphasis on the fixed works, and mostly relates to the Imperial period of the 1800s.

Some articles on the defenses of Bermuda appeared in the *Bermuda Historical Quarterly* from 1944 to 1981. This was followed by the *Bermuda Journal of Archaeology and Maritime History*, which began publication in 1989 and contains articles on the defenses, with particular reference to archaeological work, such as that which took place at Fort Cunningham in 1991–92. *The Bermuda Maritime Museum Quarterly* contains many articles on Bermuda's defenses.

Several booklets appeared in the 1990s which may be available from secondhand book stores. One was *Pillars of the Bridge*, the first publication by US forces on Bermuda. The second was a small booklet on the British defenses of the island, entitled *Great Guns of Bermuda*.

In 1997, the large book *Bermuda Forts, 1612–1957* appeared as an imprint of the Bermuda Maritime Museum Press and remains in print via the National Museum of Bermuda Press. It contains several hundred illustrations, including detailed plans of some of the forts, a chapter on the American defenses of Bermuda, and a statement on the military camps and an inventory of surviving artillery on the island. This seminal work on the defenses of Bermuda does not include the period of the Cold War.

APPENDIX: BERMUDA'S FORTS, BATTERIES, AND MILITARY RESERVATIONS

Authors' top 12[1]	Fort name[2]	Location[3]	Active period[4]	Armament[5]	Status[6]	Colonial	Imperial	20th Century
1	Dockyard, Land Front	Sandys Parish	1830–80	18 24-pdr, 2 32-pdr, 5 64-pdr RML, 2 12-pdr QFBL	Partially restored; NMB		✓	✓
1	Dockyard, the Keep	Sandys Parish	1820s, 1870s, 1890s	24 24-pdr, 6 8in., 8 32-pdr, 5 10in. RML, 8 64-pdr RML, 4 6in. BL, 3 4.7in. QFBL	Partially restored; NMB		✓	✓
1	Dockyard, Western Rampart	Sandys Parish	1840–80	14 32-pdr, 2 64-pdr RML, 1 10in. RML (1 9.2in. BL)	Partially restored; NMB		✓	
2	Fort Albert	St George's Parish	1832–1900	7 32-pdr, 2 8in. how., 2 10in. mort., 4 10in. RML	Derelict; hotel land		✓	
2	Fort Victoria	St George's Parish	1835–1935	18-24-pdr, 2-18-pdr, 8-64-pdr RML, 3-11in. RML, 2-9.2in. BL	Derelict hotel land		✓	✓
2	US Army, Fort Victoria	St George's Parish	1941–45	2 8in. railway, 2 6in. SBC, 4 90mm	Derelict; hotel land			✓
2	Western Redoubt	St George's Parish	1840s, 1890s	Not armed	Derelict; govt. land		✓	
3	Fort St Catherine	St George's Parish	1613–1900	2 6-pdr, 3 24-pdr, 12 32-pdr, 7 64-pdr, 2 64 RML, 5 10in. RML, 1 6in. BL	Museum; National Park	✓	✓	
4	St David's Battery	St George's Parish (St David's)	1910–57	2 6in. BL and 2 9.2in. BL	Stabilized; National Park			✓
5	Fort Cunningham	St George's Parish	1820s, 1870s, 1890s	10 24-pdr, 2 9in. RML, 5 10in. RML, 2 12.5in. RML	Partially restored; govt. land		✓	✓
6	Scaur Hill Fort	Sandys Parish	1870s, 1940s	2 64-pdr RML (1 64-pdr RML Moncrieff Disappearing Carriage)	Stabilized; National Park		✓	✓
6	US Army, Scaur Hill Fort	Sandys Parish	1941–45	2 8in. railway	Stabilized; National Park			✓
7	Fort George	St George's Parish	1830s, 1870s	4 24-pdr, 16 68-pdr, 2 64-pdr RML, 2 11in. RML	Harbor Radio; govt. land	✓	✓	
8	Alexandra Battery	St George's Parish	1840s–1920	5 9in. RML (1 9in. RML) and 2 6in. BL	Stabilized; National Park		✓	✓
8	Davers Fort (Gates Fort)	St George's Parish	1700s	5 12-pdr	Stabilized; National Park	✓		
9	Fort Prospect	Devonshire Parish	1870s–1900s	6 64-pdr RML	Storage area; govt. land		✓	
9	Fort Hamilton	Pembroke Parish	1870–1900	7 64-pdr RML (3 10in. RML)	Stabilized; Hamilton City Park		✓	
10	Castle Island, Devonshire Redoubt	St George's Parish	1620–1820	3 4-pdr, 4 12-pdr	Ruins; National Park	✓		
10	Castle Island, King's Castle	St George's Parish	1612–1820	3 4-pdr, 4 9-pdr, 3 12-pdr, 1 18-pdr	Ruins; National Park	✓		
10	Castle Island, Landward Fort	St George's Parish	1612–1820	1 12-pdr, 2 6-pdr, 2 9-pdr	Ruins; National Park	✓		
11	Ferry Reach, Martello Tower	St George's Parish	1822–50	1 18-pdr	Stabilized; National Park		✓	
12	Whale Bay Battery	Southampton Parish	1870s	3 9in. RML, 3 4.7in. QFBL	Stabilized; National Park		✓	✓
	Devonshire Bay Fort	Devonshire Parish	1650–1800	2 12-pdr	Ruins; National Park	✓		
	Fort Langton	Devonshire Parish	1870s–1900s	6 64-pdr RML and 3 10in. RML	Destroyed 1984; bus terminal		✓	
	Albuoy's Fort	Hamilton Parish	1620s–1811	2 9-pdr	Buried; private land	✓		
	Bailey's Bay Battery	Hamilton Parish	1600s–1870s	2 4-pdr	Buried; private land	✓		
	Charles Fort	Hamilton Parish	1615–1800	2 6-pdr	Washed away in 1960s	✓		
	Fort Bruere	Hamilton Parish	1780–84	Not armed	Ruins; private land	✓		
	Newton's Bay Battery	Hamilton Parish	1600s–1811	2 6-pdr	Buried; private land	✓		

Authors' top 12[1]	Fort name[2]	Location[3]	Active period[4]	Armament[5]	Status[6]	Colonial	Imperial	20th Century
	US Army, Base-end, Paynter's Hill	Hamilton Parish	1942–45	Fire Control Station	Derelict; govt. land			✓
	Centre Bay Fort	Paget Parish	1650–1800	2 36-pdr	Buried; private land	✓		
	Crow Lane Battery	Paget Parish	1870s	Mobile 40-pdr RML	Buried; private land		✓	
	Crow Lane Fort	Paget Parish	1650–1800	2 3-pdr, 2 6-pdr	Buried; private land	✓		
	Hungry Bay Fort	Paget Parish	1650–1800	2 12-pdr	Ruins; private land	✓		
	West Elbow Bay Fort	Paget Parish	1620–1820	2 6-pdr	Ruins; private land	✓		
	Daniel's Island Fort	Sandys Parish	1650–1820	3 6-pdr	Ruins; National Park	✓		
	King's Point Redoubt	Sandys Parish	1820s	Not armed	Buried; private land		✓	
	Mangrove Bay Fort	Sandys Parish	1650–1820	2 6-pdr	Buried; private land	✓		
	Maria Hill Fort	Sandys Parish	1790–1830	7 9-pdr, 5 18-pdr, 2 32-pdr	Buried; private land		✓	
	US Army, Base-end, Daniel's Head	Sandys Parish	1942–45	Fire Control Station	Derelict; govt. land			✓
	US Army, Base-end, Gibbs Hill	Sandys Parish	1942–45	Fire Control Station	Derelict; govt. land			✓
	US Navy, Naval Operating Base	Sandys Parish	1941–95	Naval Air Station and Base, Anti-Aircraft Battery	Destroyed; govt. land			✓
	Wreck Hill Fort	Sandys Parish	1650–1820	2 18-pdr	Ruins; private land	✓		
	Harris's Bay Fort	Smith's Parish	1620s–1811	1 8-pdr	Buried; private land	✓		
	Sear's Fort	Smith's Parish	1793–1820	1 6-pdr	Ruins; private land	✓		
	Church Bay East Fort	Southampton Parish	1650–1820	2 9-pdr	Buried; National Park	✓		
	Church Bay West Fort	Southampton Parish	1650–1820	2 12-pdr	Buried; National Park	✓		
	Fort Newbold	Southampton Parish	1650–1820	2 9-pdr	Ruins; National Park	✓		
	Hunt's Fort	Southampton Parish	1650–1820	2 3-pdr, 2 6-pdr	Buried; private land	✓		
	US Army, Tudor Hill Battery	Southampton Parish	1942–46	2 6in. SBC (Battery No. 283)	Derelict; govt. land			✓
	US Army, Turtle Hill Battery	Southampton Parish	1941–45	2 155mm GPF	Panama Mount; hotel			✓
	Warwick Camp Battery	Southampton Parish	1890s–1940s	2 6in. RBL	Derelict; govt. land			✓
	West Side Fort	Southampton Parish	1650–1820	2 6-pdr, 2 18-pdr	Ruins; private land	✓		
	Amberfish Hole Fort	St George's Parish	1700s	1 6-pdr	Buried; private land	✓		
	Buildings Bay Battery	St George's Parish	1820s	7 23pdr	Destroyed by Alexandra Battery		✓	
	Buildings Bay Fort	St George's Parish	1700s	1 6-pdr	Destroyed by buildings Bay Battery	✓		
	Coney Island Fort	St George's Parish	1790s	Not armed	Buried; govt. land		✓	
	Eastside Fort	St George's Parish	1700s	1 6-pdr	Buried; private land	✓		
	Ferry Reach, Burnt Point Fort	St George's Parish	1650–1820	5 6-pdr	Ruins; National Park		✓	
	Ferry Reach, Ferry Island Fort	St George's Parish	1790–1830	3 12-pdr, 1 18-pdr	Ruins; National Park		✓	
	Ferry Reach, Magazine	St George's Parish	1820–30	Not armed	Ruins; National Park		✓	
	Fort Clinton	St George's Parish	1700s	5 6-pdr	Buried; private land	✓		
	Moore's Fort	St George's Parish	1612–19	3 6-pdr	Burned down in 1619	✓		
	New Redoubt	St George's Parish	1700s	2 6-pdr	Buried; private land	✓		
	Paget Fascine Battery	St George's Parish	1790s	3 12-pdr	Destroyed by Upper Paget Fort	✓		
	Paget Fort	St George's Parish	1612–1820	4 6-pdr, 2 12-pdr	Ruins; National Park	✓		
	Pembroke Fort	St George's Parish	1615–29	3 6-pdr	Destroyed by hurricane in 1629	✓		
	Peniston's Redoubt	St George's Parish	1615–1800	1 6-pdr	Ruins; National Park	✓		

Authors' top 12[1]	Fort name[2]	Location[3]	Active period[4]	Armament[5]	Status[6]	Colonial	Imperial	20th Century
	Smith's Fort	St George's Parish	1613–1820	5 6-pdr	Ruins; National Park	✓		
	Southampton Fort	St George's Parish	1621–1820	5 6-pdr	Ruins; National Park	✓		
	Tobacco Bay Fort	St George's Parish	1700–1820	1 6-pdr	Buried; private land	✓		
	Town Cut Battery (Gate's Fort)	St George's Parish	1700–1820	3 12-pdr	Stabilized; National Park	✓		
	Town Redoubt No. 2	St George's Parish	1790s	2 18-pdr	Buried; private land	✓		
	Town Redoubt No. 3	St George's Parish	1790s	2 18-pdr	Buried; private land	✓		
	Town Redoubt No. 4	St George's Parish	1790s	2 18-pdr	Buried; private land	✓		
	Tucker's Town Battery	St George's Parish	1820s	2 6-pdr	Buried; private land	✓		
	Upper Paget Fort	St George's Parish	1790–1830	2 4-pdr, 2 24-pdr, 1 8in.	Destroyed by Fort Cunningham		✓	
	US Army, Cooper's Island Battery	St George's Parish	1941–45	2 155mm GPF	Destroyed; govt. land			✓
	Warwick Castle	St George's Parish	1613–1820	3 6-pdr	Replaced by Western Redoubt	✓		
	Fort Popple	St George's Parish (St David's)	1783–1806	2 9-pdr, 2 6-pdr	Derelict National Park	✓		
	US Army, Base-end, St David's	St George's Parish (St David's)	1942–45	Fire Control Station	Stabilized; National Park			✓
	US Army, Fort Bell-Kindley Field	St George's Parish (St David's)	1941–95	Airfield, anti-aircraft battery, and support	Destroyed; govt. land			✓
	Common Land Battery	Warwick Parish	1650–1820	1 9-pdr, 1 18-pdr	Buried; govt. land	✓		
	Great Turtle Bay Battery	Warwick Parish	1650–1820	2 3-pdr	Buried; govt. land	✓		
	Heron Bay Fort	Warwick Parish	1650–1820	2 6-pdr, 1 18-pdr	Buried; govt. land	✓		
	Jobsons Cove Fort	Warwick Parish	1650–1820	5 4-pdr, 1 6-pdr	Buried; govt. land	✓		
	Jobsons Fort	Warwick Parish	1620–1820	2 4-pdr, 2 12-pdr	Buried; govt. land	✓		
	US Army, AATC	Warwick Parish	1942–45	Various WW2 anti-aircraft guns	Destroyed; govt. land			✓

Notes
[1] Author's ranking of the "best" 12 fortifications on Bermuda (for visitors to use).
[2] Name of the Fort or Battery or Military Reservation – only listed ones that had artillery.
[3] By parish.
[4] In years – from the construction to discontinuation of military use.
[5] Armament mounted throughout the active period; bold items indicate surviving artillery on site.
[6] Current status of site (condition and ownership).

Fort Victoria shown in 1990 after the construction of a hotel resort on the fort's grounds, with a swimming pool and nightclub replacing the Bombproof Keep. By this date, the hotel had already been closed for many years, only to be demolished in 2008. Note the surviving 9.2in. gun, with its barrel aiming through the hotel's lobby. (McGovern Collection)

INDEX

Figures in **bold** refer to illustrations.

Admiralty House 37, 58
aircraft 53, **53**, **54**, 55
Alexandra (Buildings Bay) Battery **27**
  armament 26–27, 38, 40, 42–44, 56, **58**
  design 20
  nowadays 59
  post-military uses 57
  summary 61, 62
American Civil War (1861–65) 38
American War of Independence (1775–83)
  18, 36
Anglo-Boer War (1899–1902) 52–53
Anti-Motor Torpedo Boat Battery 48
Argus Island **54**, 55
armament
  20th-century developments 41–42, 56–57
  155mm guns **48**
anti-aircraft artillery 49, **49**
  barbette guns **48**
  cannons **A** (15)
  fort by fort summary 61–63
  Imperial period 21–36, 38–40
  RBLs 57, **58**
  RMLs **1**, **55**, 59
  US emplacements 46–50, **G** (51)

Battery Construction No. 283 48, 58
Battery Construction No. 284 48, **48**, **G**
  (51), 57, **60**
Bermuda
  geography 4–5
  harbors 5
  history 5–7, 10, 14–17, 18, 38–41, 52–55
  maps **4**, **5**, **11**, **19**, **43**
  place names 5
  strategic significance 4, 18
Bermuda Dockyard see Royal Naval
  (Bermuda) Dockyard
Bermuda Militia Artillery **49**
Bermúdez, Juan de 10
Blanshard, Major 22
boats see ships and boats
Boaz Island 52, 53
Boer War see Anglo-Boer War
Buildings Bay Battery see Alexandra
  (Buildings Bay) Battery
Burnt Point Fort **17**, 62
Butler, Nathaniel 14

Canadian troops 49, 50, 52, 53, 54, 55
Castle (Southampton) Harbour 13–14, **A**
  (15), **16**
Charles Fort 12, 13, 61
Clarence Barracks 37
Cold War 41, **53**, 54–55
Cooper's Island 13, 42, 46, 48, 49, 56

Daniel's Head 49, 54, **56**, 62
Darrell's Island 50, **50**, 52
Davers Fort see Gates (Davers) Fort
Devonshire Redoubt 10, 13, **16**, 61
Durnford, Major Andrew 13, 16, 18, 21, 27

Fort Albert (Eastern Redoubt) 23–24, 38,
  40, 55, 57, 59, 61
Fort Bell 42, 52–54, **53**, 55, 58, 63
Fort Cunningham **28**, **E** (39)

armament 27–29, 38, 40, 42–44, 56, 59
  design 27–29
  nowadays 59
  post-military uses 57
  summary 61
Fort George 21–22, **23**, 38, 40, 57, 59, 61
Fort Hamilton 32, 34, **34**, 40, 58, 59, 61
Fort Langton 32, 34, 40, 50, 58, 61
Fort Prospect 32, 34, **37**, 40, 58, 59, 61
Fort St Catherine **26**
  armament 20, 24–26, 38, 40, **55**
  design 12, 20
  nowadays 59
  post-military uses 57
  summary 61
Fort Victoria **23**, **B** (25), 57, **63**
  under Americans 49
  armament **1**, 23, 42–44, 38, 40, 56, 57
  design 22–23
  nowadays 59
  post-military uses 57
  summary 61
Fort William see Western Redoubt
Furbert, Lance **60**

garrison life 14–16, 36–37, 50–52
Gates (Davers) Fort **17**, 57, 59, 61
Greenslade, Admiral John W. 42

HMS Malabar 54, 57
Hughes, Lieutenant Gerald Rickards **1**
Hurd, Lieutenant Thomas 18

James, Captain Jules 46
Jervois, Colonel W. Drummond 20–21, 24,
  26, 32, 34–36

Kindley Field 53
  armament 49
  history 42, 52, 53–54, 55
  nowadays 58, 59
  summary 63
King's Castle 10, 13, 16, **16**, 61

Landward Fort 13–14, **16**, 61

Marchant Tupper, Gaspard le: paintings by
  20, 26
Martello Tower 21, **22**, 38, 57, 61
militia 14, 16, 37
Moore, Richard 10, 12, 13
Moore's Fort 13, 62
Moore's Mount 16

National Museum of Bermuda **31**, 44, 57,
  58, 59

operational history 16–17, 38–40, 52–55

Paget Fort 10, 12, 16, 59, 62
Pembroke Fort 12, 13, 62
Peniston's Redoubt 12–13, 62
Prospect Camp 37, **37**, 58, 59
Prospect Hill Position 32–34

Retreat Hill 21, 22, **23**, 59
Robinson, Sir Robert 14
Royal Garrison Artillery **40**

Royal Naval (Bermuda) Dockyard **31**
  armament 29–36, 38, 40, 45, 46, 56, **56**
  defenses 20–21, **20**, 29–36, **C** (33), **D**
    (35), 44, 45–46, 49, 50
  final days 41, 52, 53, 54
  Floating Dock **6**
  garrison 37
  history 6, 18–20, 29
  importance as likely objective of enemy
    attack 41
  Keep 29, 31–32, **D** (35), **46**, 59, 61
  maps **19**
  nowadays 58, 59
  summary 61

St David's Battery **F** (47)
  armament 42–45, **44**, 56
  nowadays 59
  post-military uses 52, 57
  summary 61
St George's Garrison 37, 57
Scaur Hill Fort **36**
  armament 36, 40, 48, 56
  design 21, 36
  nowadays 58, 59
  summary 61
seaplanes 53, **53**, 54
Seven Years' War (1756–63) 16
ships and boats, as defenses 16, 50, 53
Smith's Fort 10, 12, **13**, 59, 63
Somers, Admiral Sir George 10
Somerset Position 36, **36**
Southampton Fort 10, 14, **A** (15), 59, 63
Southampton Harbour see Castle
  (Southampton) Harbour
Spain, engagements against 16
Strong, Colonel Alden G. 46
submarines 41, 50, **52**, 53, 54, 55

Tudor Hill 48, 49, 55, 56, 62
Turtle Hill **48**, 49, 56, 62

Upper Paget Fort 27, 63
US Naval Air Station 42, 50, 53, 58, 59
US Naval Operating Base 42, 49. 52, 53,
  58, 62
USA
  Bermudan operational history 52–55
  early desire to possess Bermuda 20
  fortifications created by 42, 46–50, 56–57
  primary defense of Bermuda taken over by
    41, 42

War of the Spanish Succession (1701–14) 16
Warwick Camp 37, 45–46, 56, 58, 59, 62
Warwick Castle 10, 12, 63
Western Redoubt (Fort William) 22, 38, 57,
  59, 61
Whale Bay Battery **45**
  armament 36, 40, 44, 45, 56
  design 21, 34–36
  nowadays 58, 59
  summary 61
White, Major D.G. 42
Willock, Colonel Roger 60
World War 1 (1914–18) 41, 50, 53
World War 2 (1939–45) 41, 42, 46–50,
  50–52, 53–54